OFFENSIVE COMPASSION

24 ACTIONS YOU CAN DO TODAY TO COMBAT HATE IN THE REAL WORLD

MELLISA SHERLIN

Cerulean Streak Media

Lowell

Cerulean Streak Media
63 13th Street, Suite 508
Lowell, Massachusetts 01850

Copyright © 2017 by Mellisa Sherlin

ALL RIGHTS RESERVED, including the right to reproduce this book or portions thereof in any form whatsoever without written permission by the publisher. For information address Cerulean Streak Media, 63 13th Street, Suite 508, Lowell, MA 01850.

For information about special discounts for bulk purchases, please contact Offensive Compassion at 978.390.1139 or staff@offensive-compassion.com.

To learn more about how to use healthy communication to effectively create and sustain the life you want to be living, or to Mellisa Sherlin speak to your group; other live events; or additional helpful resources on simple things you can do today please contact Offensive Compassion at 978.390.1139 or visit the website www.Offensive-Compassion.com.

Front cover designed by Offensive Compassion.
Text design and typography by Cerulean Streak Media.
Figures design by Mellisa Sherlin.

Manufactured in the United States of America.

ISBN 978-0-9996598-0-9

Please Note: While this compilation of tips and activities have been used successfully by the author, total success in reproducing the skills herein are not guaranteed. The author has complied the information contained herein from a variety of sources and neither the author, publisher, manufacturers, nor distributions can assume responsibility for the effectiveness of the suggested activities. Caution is urged while taking action. No warranty or representation is made by Cerulean Streak Media or Offensive Compassion with respect to the outcome of any of the actions described in this book. Cerulean Streak Media and Offensive Compassion shall have no liability for damages, (whether direct, indirect, consequential, or otherwise) arising from the use, attempted used of application of any activities described in this book.

OFFENSIVE COMPASSION

24 ACTIONS YOU CAN DO TODAY
TO COMBAT HATE
IN THE REAL WORLD

for Waterman

Table of Contents

Forward – A Case for Compassion

1 What is Compassion and Why Bother
  Pain Makes Us Selfish 3
  All Pain is Caused by Unmet Needs 4
  What I Learned Trolling Hate Groups 6

2 The 5 Steps to a Healthy Conversation
  Basics of Healthy Communication 20
  How to Have a Healthy Conversation 23

3 Recognize and Dismantle Blocking Techniques
  Dismantling These Blocking Techniques 32
  Find Common Ground with Reflective Listening 33

4 Stages of Grief, Learning, and Change
  Stage One 39
  Stage Two 40
  Stage Three 41
  Stage Four 42
  Stage Five 43
  Moving Through These Processes 45

5 Action Recipes
  # 1: Notice Your Feelings and Needs 49
  # 2: Know your Preferred Patterns 53
  # 3: Keep Your Self Promises 61
  # 4: Do Something You Enjoy 67

# 5: Reduce Your Irritations	73
# 6: Use Positive Descriptions	79
# 7: Find a New Favorite	85
# 8: Stay in the Moment	91
# 9: Look for Humanity	97
# 10: Use Cheat Sheets	103
# 11: Allow Yourself to Learn	109
# 12: Prepare for Tomorrow	117
# 13: Set Your Intentions	123
# 14: Set Healthy Expectations	129
# 15: Use Empathy	135
# 16: Take a Moment to be a Hero	141
# 17: Make Eye Contact	147
# 18: Give a Genuine Compliment	153
# 19: Say Hello to Your Neighbors	159
# 20: Creative Inclusive Space	165
# 21: Express Your Disagreements Safely	171
# 22: Disrupt Anger Safely	179
# 23: Compassion Flyers	189
# 24: Kindness Challenge	195

6 Additional Resources for Select Action Recipes

List of Emotions	201
List of Needs	204
# 2: Know Your Preferred Patterns Tracker	206
# 4: Do Something You Enjoy Idea Sheet	207
# 5: Reduce Your Irritations Guide	208
# 8: Stay in the Moment Sample Worksheet	210
# 16: Take a Moment to Be a Hero Ideas	211
# 23: Compassion Flyers Ideas and Samples	214
# 24: The Kindness Challenge Sample	218

7   Notes from the Other Side of Learning
    Express Your Style 222
    The Five Communication Styles 223
    Recognizing the Different Communication Styles ... 231
    Encouragement for the Low Points 232

About the Author 236

Recommended Reading List 237

Before You Start

Each purchase of *Offensive Compassion*, helps provide similar trainings to women rebuilding their lives. We're so glad you bought this book. You really bought two books. You have your copy, and one copy is given to a woman living in a shelter. Your purchase of this book, or any other services at our website, Offensive-Compassion.com, allows us to provide communication training and assistance to others who need this valuable information to create and sustain a life they want to life.

The information presented in this book was first shared with a group of six courageous women living in a shelter rebuilding their lives after trauma. It was the first time any of them had heard about healthy communication and how to use it. This new tool worked brilliantly for each of them. The successes of those first students helped spread the class to 27 shelters in the Merrimack Valley of Massachusetts and New Hampshire within four years.

People outside of these shelters wanted this information too, and this book was born. Staying true to our commitment to help courageous women rebuilding their lives, each purchase you make of this book or from our website provides a similar item to a courageous woman rebuilding her life.

To show our appreciation and dedication to making sure these skills will work in your life, we are giving you worksheets and templates to strengthen your understanding of the elements shared on these pages.

www.Offensive-Compassion.com/resources.html.

Follow us on social media so you can hear about all the newest events, classes, books, and downloads to support your growing compassion at www.facebook.com/Offensive-Compassion.

How to Use This Book

Technology changes, and the specific tools for achieving specific objectives change. People do not change, and the simple communication skills and principles presented in this book are timeless. For that reason, we do not discuss specific businesses or technologies in this book as the information would become out of date before publication.

For timely advice on how use the current technologies as you discover your talents for effecting change, please visit our website http://www.Offensive-Compassion.com.

When you see this symbol in the margin, more information on the topic is available on our website. On the website, you can also  join our email list to have additional resources delivered right to your inbox.

This book is intended as a primer to encourage you to include compassion towards yourself and others in your daily actions. All information presented in this book is presented as an introduction to the topics, and in no way, presents a comprehensive study of the topics. Further information is available on all of these ideas presented within.

We encourage you to continue learning about healthy communication, techniques to express yourself effectively while remaining kind, and other activities you can engage in to spread love in the real world.

You may want to grab a notebook and work your way through this book, page by page. Take notes, and share your discoveries with us. We are always looking for new ways to express compassion as we affect positive change.

Life is an experiment. The more things you try, the more things you learn about yourself and those around you. Every action has been tried, tested and proven successful by many people before you. In that learning process, common pitfalls have been discovered.

To assist you in avoiding those slippery spots on the learning curve, we have provided warning and caution points to alert you to the places others have stumbled, and what they learned in order to make this work.

> ### *Watch Your Step*
> When you see this box, the information inside was helpful to those who came this way before you.

As you progress through the information, be kind to yourself. Whether this idea of healthy communication and active compassion are alien concepts or if you pride yourself on your communication prowess, learning to use new skills is difficult. We can only use the skills we have learned about. Be kind to yourself as you learn. Kindness is the only way to make it stick.

FORWARD
A Case for Compassion

Why?

I WROTE THIS book to do something. I'm not sure what that something was when I started. You see, hurting people have inundated me with requests to help them "get through this". The trainings I lead on healthy communication turned into support groups for traumatized survivors pulled back into the fray before they were ready.

First, this book was a wallet sized cheat sheet. Then it became a tri-fold pamphlet. From there, the information grew into a white sheet. After that, I relented, and wrote quick essay and how-to. My initial idea of a small 40 or 50-page eBook exploded into a 250-page book, worksheets, a companion workbook and a slew of online resources growing with every passing month.

Why?

Communication is not an innate human skill. Speaking is. Making sounds and gestures are. The desire to communicate with a group is an innate desire, but the skills to achieve this need are a learned behavior.

Communication is a learned skill passed among family members. Our families introduce us to language and set our standards for communication and group interactions. If your family uses those tools ineffectively, you are trained in using these tools ineffectively. If your family uses this skill well, you learn effective communication skills.

The skills we use to communicate strengthen our family and community bonds. If your family uses healthy communication skills, you are welcome into the larger group of people using healthy communication skills. If your family uses unhealthy communication skills, you are accepted into the larger group of people using unhealthy communication skills. And when you wander either intentionally or unintentionally into contact with a group using the "other" skill set, there is friction.

At one point, generations ago, this malicious use of language was tolerated by society. Now, with instant access to other groups, other perspectives, and other communication techniques, it is not. Yes, older generations "have always" felt friction with the newer generations. It's different now.

Why?

Our system of government is based on the "enlightened" idea that logic and reason lead debates on ideas to bring about the best solution for the masses. The United States of America has forgotten how to engage in this required healthy dialogue. Our citizens and the people we elect to represent us, have stopped reaching for consensus. Instead we reach of safety, hunkering down in our smaller and smaller communities and families.

In this self-sorting into smaller and more cloistered groups of those who agree with us, we have avoided using the skills needed to reach consensus. Now that we need those skills, the average person has no experience to draw from when presented with a dissenting idea or contradictory solution to current issues. We have turned into a country of small individual groups cutting each other down to allow our group the immediate advantage. We are using self-sorting to solve our problems instead of self-reflection to see how our actions could contrite to and solve the problems.

Why?

I wrote this book to share my methods for "getting through to people" who disagree with me. I learned all of these communication skills as an adult. They are not shared in my family, and all those methods I use to get through to people who disagree with me are methods honed through my various attempts to make myself understood to a family who wants nothing more than to crush my soul.

The contents of this book congealed slowly. Then events happened in the United States of America which scared, angered and eventually motivated people to take action. The actions taken were lacking one very important element for success and sustainability. Those actions were missing compassion for those who disagree with us.

Each and every one of these techniques I share in this book, I have used with varying degrees of success with in my own family. This lack of success within my own family, lead me to seek out other groups.

This book is not for those wanting to crush or punish their opponent on the path to victory. That kind of thinking got us into this problem. This book is for those who are searching for a way to understand what these "others" are thinking as they watch the same events you watch, but come to significantly different solutions to the problems you see. Yes, you can read that as don't see a problem.

Why?

Through years of teaching women the skills they need to effectively communicate in order to create and sustain the life they want to live, I have been privy to countless acts of courage, love and compassion.

This is book is an act of resistance to the hate and fear swirling around. Everything in this book has been tested both online and in person to successfully defuse and then understand the people who disagree with me. I hope these actions are as useful for you.

CHAPTER 1
What is Compassion and Why Bother

When I teach the idea of compassion in a class, I start with: "Compassion is a lot like getting out of bed. Some days it's easier than others." But, those ladies know what they signed up for, and the analogy works to set the stage for the work we are about to do together.

Dictionary Definition of Compassion

Compassion (kəm-păsh'ən), noun, is the deep feeling of sharing the suffering of another; mercy derived from the Latin word *compati* meaning to sympathize with.

This official definition of compassion is not how I understand the concept. I think of compassion as a verb. Maybe my dictionary is out of date; it's been on every incarnation of my desk since 1989. Probably July of 1989, since that is when my edition of The American Heritage Dictionary was published. Online dictionaries have other slightly different definitions.

> *Dictionary.com Definition of Compassion*
>
> Compassion (kəmˈpaSHən), noun, is the sympathetic pity and concern for the sufferings or misfortunes of others.

The explanations of the meaning are similar, but very different. At least, the two sources agree on how to pronounce the word. The truth is, there is no universal definition of compassion. The idea is a moving target or goal instead of a finite point. The way we express this idea grows and changes as we do. And our definition of compassion is a unique as our styles of expression.

Compassion is inclusive. It is being able to see another person's completely different perspective objectively. Then instead of assuming the person did whatever it was intentionally because they are inherently assholes who enjoy hurting others, Compassion assumes everyone is inherently a good person who has really good reasons for doing what they did. This idea can be really hard to buy into, especially if you have been hurt or are hurting.

> *Compassion is a lot like getting out of bed. Some days it's easier than others.*

Compassion is realizing you have good intentions, even if things didn't work out the way you imagined they would. No matter the outcome, you had a good reason for choosing the actions you did. You thought the action would provide what you wanted or needed in a situation.

Other people have the same needs as you do. They make choices to get those needs met, just like you do. Everyone make similar choices based on past similar experiences with a given situation. These choices are designed to have our needs met.

Compassion looks to see what need a person was filling when they did whatever hurt or disappointed you or others in the past.

Pain Makes Us Selfish

Pain hurts. Pain hurts, because something in our life is not right. The sensation of pain gets out attention, and hold that attention until the pain goes away. Pain motivates us to get stuff done, if only to get rid of the pain. Pain makes us selfish in order to figure out what is hurting and make it stop.

People only chose actions they can perceive.

When someone is in pain, their attention is drawn to the pain. Their choices are made to end the pain, lessen the pain or at very least, distract them from the pain. We have all been in pain. We know the sensation.

This pain limits the number of options we can see. This is why people in pain make poor choices. Then those poor choices compound to limit the options people can choose from. It is a vicious cycle. The only way out is compassion. Compassion with yourself by taking a slightly better choice than you wanted to. That slightly better choice will open up more slightly better options. Eventually, those slightly better choices compound to create good choices. If you see others in pain, making poor choices, demanding they choose what you see, is impossible. Help them choose slightly better choices.

Our largest regrets are related to things we did or didn't do while we were in pain. Look back at all the things in your life you are not proud of. You made choices that didn't work out. Those choices may have been conscious in the moment, or they may have been unconsciously following what we thought was the "right thing to do" in the moment.

Selfishness is a result of pain. All pain stems from our needs not being met.

All Pain is Caused by Unmet Needs

We have all felt pain. Pain hurts. Many people have dedicated their lives to exploring what is pain and how is it created. There is a well-respected idea in psychology called Maslow's Hierarchy of Needs. Abraham Maslow believed people have a set of motivation systems separate from the, then popular, idea of behaviors motivated only by rewards (like Pavlov and his dogs) or by unconscious desires (like Freud and his obsession with mommy issues). Maslow believed that people are motivated to reach self-actualization, but are blocked from that ultimate life goal when our needs are not met. He believed only after the most basic needs are filled can a person attempt to fill less concrete needs and effectively contribute to society we live in.

His theory has been modified a bit over the years, but basically it looks like a pyramid with Basic Needs at the base, Psychological Needs in the middle, and Self-Fulfillment Needs at the top. When the needs are not met, pain keeps us from moving up the pyramid to our higher goals.

Maslow divided our needs into five categories. At the bottom are our physiological needs. Next step up is our needs for safety. Once those are met, we can start to fill our need for belonging and love. After we are secure in our community, we can tend to our esteem needs, of being appreciated as a contributing member of society. At the very top of Maslow's pyramid of needs is self-actualization, where we have reached our larger goals and give back to those still working their way up the pyramid.

This pyramid served the idea well, but who wants to hold off until everything is perfect before helping others. Needs are innate and are with us every moment of our lives. When needs are met, we focus on other things. When needs are not met, we get selfish.

> *Holding off filling needs until the basics are out of the way, makes everything hurt more.*

We have all met people who are struggling to meet their basic needs, but still show kindness and compassion to others. This is because they have met other needs in different part of this pyramid. I like the hierarchy, because it shows why some needs hurt more than others. The more basic needs you have ignored, the harder it is to meet the innate needs further up. You can, but takes more work.

Our Seven Innate Needs

Connection: Being part of a group.

Play: Fun, laugher, enjoyment

Honesty: Integrity, truth, self-worth.

Physical Well-Being: Food, water, shelter, rest

Peace: Calm, and healthy interdependence.

Autonomy: Ability to choose and follow our own dreams.

Meaning: a larger purpose than ourselves, spirituality, and community.

What I Learned Trolling Hate Groups

This book grew out of experience. It was compiled out of necessity. And it is being shared with you out of an undying belief that we can choose better.

The evening of November 9, 2017, there was a loud gathering in an open field just outside my city home. I didn't know what was going on, and I didn't want to know. It was past 10 PM after a shocking defeat of my candidate of choice. I wanted to turn off the election returns and get some sleep before dealing with this confusing situation. Recount?

My doorbell rang. The dog barked. I went to answer it. A man I recognized as a neighbor stood on my steps. We mow our lawns at the same time. He took his nephews trick-or-treating a couple weeks ago. I turned on the porch light. He looked happy. Maybe the recount was already announced?

I opened the door more hopeful than I had felt in hours. "Hi! What's up?" I asked.

He was wearing an armband over top of a long sleeve collared shirt. There was a swastika on his armband. But it wasn't Halloween. We mowed our lawns at the same time. How could my neighbor have a swastika? How could he wear it outside even if it was dark? How could he be smiling wearing a swastika? Why is he knocking on my door wearing a swastika?

He gestured to the loud gathering in the field across the street with his other arm. "We're having a party!" he told me. "Want to come?"

Those words didn't make sense. I followed his gesture towards the crowd. There was more than one person over there, maybe twenty people. A car drove up the street and parked on the curb beside the field less than 10 car spaces from my house. He wasn't the only one on the sidewalk at this hour either. Sporadic groups of people were making their way up the steep hill of my city street. Two groups had coolers. A couple with a kid swinging between their hands. These people were happy. These people were going to a party less than 10 car spaces from my home.

I looked back at my neighbor. His expression changed. Probably because mine did. "No!" was all I could manage to get past the shock. My dog barked fiercely at my tone.

I heard my neighbor cursing at me. He called me, "… a traitor to your race…" as I slammed the door. The door stuck a bit in the lower left corner. I kicked it shut and locked to door.

The group partied out there until the police came around midnight or 1 AM. I found out later, other neighbors called the police. The group didn't have a permit to use the grassy "park space" and were asked to disband. I did nothing. I hid in my room as Nazis partied next to my house.

> *A good neighbor knocked on my door wearing a swastika, and I froze.*

The next day was Wednesday. I was still reeling from the day before: the election results; the fact a Nazi lived on my street; I considered a swastika wearing Nazi a "good neighbor"; and the fact I was a complete coward last night, hiding in my room and crying into my dog's soft coat. Shame made it hard to brush my teeth, but I had a class to teach. I had to be stronger now. I had to function in this topsy-turvy world where all those paranoid whispers were proven true on my doorstep in the dark of night.

I didn't want to function in a world where Nazis were so happy with election results they partied across the street from my house. I dreaded the day to come and the possible days that followed. Paramount in my thoughts was how I could inspire the women I worked with to be courageous, use these communication skills I was teaching them to build and sustain the life they wanted when just last night I was a coward and words failed me. I didn't want to live here.

That weekly class didn't cover any of the prepared curriculum. Instead, the group of women talked about the election, what it meant to them, and expressed their crushing fear about the future. Yes, crushing fear. These women were homeless, without driver's licenses, no savings, no bank accounts, unemployed and in varying degrees of physically healing after escaping with children from violent situations. My courageous women had hit the proverbial rock bottom, crashed through it to an even worse low, and were in the process of rebuilding the foundations of their lives. They didn't have the emotional band width to deal with growing violence they witnessed around them. They didn't have the luxury of money for food let alone an apartment or the ability to emigrate to Canada. These courageous women found themselves trapped in a new situation where they were the easy targets of abuse.

> *Watch Your Step*
>
> Humans assume we would all make the same choices, but we all have different experiences which shape those choices.

Instead of teaching, I listened and assured them the healthy communication techniques and tools covered in this 10-week course would help them deal with this hate. The course focused on the Five Steps of a Healthy Conversation and how to apply them in stressful situations… dealing with the structure of the shelter, getting along with co-workers, handling difficult family dynamics, and advocating for their kids.

To them, my ideas of healthy communication and compassion were "great in theory" but "don't really work in the real world". These ladies had some success applying these new skills in very specific instances, but didn't know how to apply these useful skills to their daily life in "the real world". My ladies demanded proof this new skill was what they needed.

Faced with their panic, they needed demonstrable proof these techniques of healthy communication and the healthy expression of compassion work today in this terrible new world they perceived. Nebulous examples of this skill working in the past were no longer valid. Their world had flipped, and they needed to see concrete examples of turning toxic communication into healthy communication to trust these alien skills.

Their demand was a tall order. They needed this to trust their teacher, but I needed it to trust the world. I knew healthy communication worked. I knew I had used these skills to deal with very manipulative, violent people. I knew I had used and shared this information with those around me so well I no longer had to deal with people using unhealthy communication tactics on a daily basis. I didn't know where to find pockets of unhealthy communication.

Thursday, there was a flyer on my porch when I got home. No swastikas. I didn't know what the harsh eagle meant at the time. I saw a smiling stereotypical white family, a young mom, a dad, and elementary age kids, the daughter was younger. "Preserve American Culture. Join us and make America Great Again." I puked a little. White nationalists were close enough to walk over and touch my house when I wasn't there. White nationalists were so emboldened by the President Elect, they were out distributing flyers in the middle of the day. They were so confident in their hatred, someone put contact info on the flyer. It was a garbled Hotmail account and a cellphone. The anonymous accounts gave me some solace; the creators were still hiding in the shadows.

Call it what you will: Extreme naiveté; Morbid curiosity; Channeled rage… I emailed. These were the monsters hiding under the bed. I had no intention of making friends or even peace with the monsters. I wanted to see how many were down there, then destroy them.

That's not something you put into an introductory email. After hours of crafting the best I could come up with was: "Hi. I saw your flyer on [my street]. Do you have a FB page? – Miss"

My neighbor had called me "a traitor" two nights before. Hitting send, I felt like a traitor. I didn't get a reply for two days. Saturday, November 12, 2016.

Five days before my kid's 12th birthday, I joined my first hate group.

What I learned trolling hate groups with healthy communication, has been boiled down to the activities in this book. Interacting with people in such a cloistered and vindictive pit was emotionally, physically and spiritually painful for me. The lessons I learned were worth the growing pains. The main takeaways from that experience are provided below.

> *Takeaway #1*
>
> **Social Media is not a conversation.**

No matter which platform you choose, there are posts. These posts sit somewhere. Other people read the crumbs of someone else's thought processes, and post their own commentary inspired by what they read. This is not a real conversation. It is stripped down communication. Social

Media is blind to vocal tone, body language, and micro expressions. All of the vital non-articulated parts of communication have been stripped away.

This stripping down of what we are trying to articulate created an intrinsic miscommunication. The miscommunication is surmountable, but at every moment, it is still there. Therefore, I did not go into the online forums looking to change anyone's point of view. I went to understand how these people could look at the same things I was seeing and come to completely different conclusions.

Every conversation I thought I had online, was not a conversation. Therefore, I decided my initial understanding of a comment was flawed. Before replying, posting or in any way being dragged down into the festering hate, I needed to clarify what was being communicated.

> *My neighbor had called me "a traitor" two nights before. Hitting send, I felt like a traitor.*

Not many people in these groups appreciated the process of achieving clarity. No matter what interaction I received, I promised myself I would not allow the comments to affect me. These people were commenting to non-entities. These posts belonged to people swinging in the dark hoping to hit something before it hit them.

> *Takeaway #2*
>
> Cloistered groups reward conformity.

The posts I waded through and littered my feeds were more than fear-mongering memes and angry vents about strangers. The posts, replied and interactions looked like any other group I was part of on social media. Some people would get 100 + comments others would get zero. The general population got 15 – 30 replies. The users shared memes, some with cats. People vented about their daily toils. Pictures of food, clothing, and social events flowed. Cruel humor took cheap shots at hurting people.

Any uncertainty or disagreement was perceived as a weakness. Members swarmed the posts with the most scathing and intentionally obtuse comments. It was like watching a feeding frenzy on Discovery Channel's Shark Week. No one stepped in to offer another perspective or defend those members being eviscerated.

All comments and replies were twisted into a form of judgment: the memes, the vents about the day, snide comments about pop culture. The memes played on fears of being rejected from their society or offered a scapegoat for their mediocrity while alluding to a predestined greatness.

I recognized this pattern. At first, I thought I was foisting this pattern onto these people who I was silently judging. But the truth bit back hard and clear with one post.

A member using an image of a woman holding a bald baby posted about her irritation that the popular store she frequented was out of the formula she needed and how driving to another store ruined her day. To me, this was a common "new parent post". In fact, a friend with a similarly aged kid vented similarly about out-of-stock baby wipes.

These two women were experiencing similar growing pains of parenthood. I commented on my friend's post, "Hugs. So frustrating. Hope your day get better." The similarity of experiences encouraged me to post the same encouragement in this hate group. My comment stuck out like a sore thumb.

The other comments were hurtful. Strangers demanded to know why she was feeding her baby formula instead of breastmilk – adding malicious lies about the production of baby formula. Others chided her for shopping at the retail outlet near her home – adding incendiary comments about people shopping there. Still more ridiculed her for running out of formula in the first place – adding hurtful assumptions about her family structure.

Mine was not the only commentary on the post. But it was the only encouraging comment she received in the five comments offered before mine. I remembered what it was like to be a new mom. I remember all those comments leveled at me. And I remember how I wished someone would have stepped in to help deflect those comments.

I jumped in. I wanted to jump in with a baseball bat and smash all the mean people attacking this flustered new parent. Instead, I looked at my monitor cluttered with sticky note cheat sheets. "Be kind."

To the *Formula Haters*, I offered congratulations on being able to produce high quality milk to feed their kids, and reminded them not everyone is so fortunate. So, formula is a necessary evil to keep kids alive. To the hateful comments I received, I redirected with questions looking to understand not convince. "Did that work for you?" "Did you take dietary supplements while you lactated?" "How long does it take to nurse your baby?" "Did your baby take to nursing right away, or did you need to do the bate-and-switch thing with yours, too?"

> *Choose kindness when you can. If you look long enough, there will be a kind option to offer.*

To the *Convenience Haters*, I agreed that I prefer a different store, too. But I did admit, I do run in to the retail giant when I am swamped with errands. After a long day, a ten-minute stop a few miles from home is more appealing than the hour plus round trip to the preferred store. This chain received more vile comments than I expected from both people who shopped at the large retailer and those who did not. Finding questions to illicit understanding was difficult without using judgmental words. "The lines in both stores are getting slower. Do you think they are competing for longest check out?" "Those impulse purchases right there kill me. Which one gets to you?"

To the *Unprepared Haters,* I congratulated their stockpiles and appreciated their sequencing abilities. My seeking to understand was really brain-picking for their household organizational tips. I'm always looking for more efficient organization tips.

Comments after my comments were kinder, more commiserating with this new parent. A day later, I checked on the chain - 45 comments. I had made a dozen myself between the hate mongers. What I discovered surprised me. The comments were kinder to this new parent. Of the comments added after my intervention, two were cruel. Each of the cruel comments had replies defending the new parent. The "Said no parent ever." was not as kind as I strove for, but it was heartening in its own right.

My one kind comment had changed the dialogue around this person's day. One kind comment paused the hate mongering for a moment.

Takeaway #3

People are in these groups.

Real humans are in these groups. People with lives, and hopes, fears and dreams posted in these groups. I went in looking for the boogie man. Instead I found Suzie Homemaker and Andy Q. Body. Posts about a new puppy and upcoming holiday preparations were sprinkled between the racist memes and fear mongering ideology. The monsters weren't just the good neighbor across the street who mowed his lawn at the same time as me. The monsters were also pushing papers for the insurance company I used for decades, and running successful restaurants. People claiming to be veterans, police and doctors posted.

> *My neighbor wasn't the anomaly among the monsters.*

When I realized real people are in these groups, the enemy transformed. My friendly neighbor wasn't the anomaly among the monsters. The monsters were the anomaly among the meek followers. Followers want to conform and hide in a group. Scared little kids who joined the bullies to avoid getting hurt themselves. Those cowardly kids grew into cowardly adults, and the monsters were still bullying them.

> *Takeaway #4*
>
> **Injecting an adult perspective is necessary.**

Humans love structure. We are social creatures, and we love structure. This instinct creates followers and leaders. Humans learn fastest when someone else model's the behavior for us. We call them role models and we look up to them.

These groups had role models, too. The popular kids who taught all the others how to play. I modeled healthy communication. I modeled compassion, even when it was hard. I didn't want to be kind to these hate spewing monsters. But, they were not monsters. These were hurting followers looking for a solution to their problems. Whatever led them down this dark path, they were being given really bad advice about how to solve their problems, i.e., blame someone else.

I got angry at the blatant disregard for facts. Parts were like watching a real-time horror movie or an awful natural disaster. The cruel interactions and violent language reminded me of my earlier years. I could have turned away. I could have left the groups. I stayed, not just because I did nothing that night as Nazis partied outside my house. I stayed for more than my scared students. I interacted for me. I put myself back into that disgusting pit of hate and blame to test myself.

As most middle class, white Americans, I had spent too much of my life looking away. Nazis partied outside my home, because I looked away and did nothing. I had to do something.

That something was the one thing in those hate groups no one was really doing. I listened for the pain. More than being heard, people want to be understood. I wanted to hear what these people were saying, and figure out what disconnect prevented us from seeing the same thing. I comforted that pain, and then I offered a different way to alleviate that unique pain.

> *Takeaway #5*
>
> We all know someone who embraces radicalized hate.

Memes from these groups spill over onto the larger communities on social media. My social media friends were classmates, courageous students, co-workers, fellow authors, creative people, and athletes with a spattering of people interested in communication and words. I didn't expect anything found circulating in these pits of hate to show up in my real newsfeeds from the like-minded friends I had gathered over the years. A former coworker shared a meme and shattered the imaginary line I had drawn across my Facebook feed.

The meme was a picture of a woman yelling at someone or thing while standing on what looked like a subway platform. She was wearing a black headscarf. Big block letters questioned her citizenship and her right to express herself in public. When this meme showed up on three of the four hate groups I infiltrated, it got dozens of likes and a handful of affirmative comments whenever it made the rounds. Those festering hate groups introduced the meme with either a derogatory comment about her perceived spiritual preferences or dismissed her citizenship. Someone I worked with for years introduced the photo by demanding she "shut up and go home."

A person I knew, a person I interacted with most week days for years, just parroted hate-speak from the bowels of social media. His post had garnered five likes and three comments before it invaded my feed.

"Truth!"
"You say it -----."
"I bet her husband beats her."
"Serves her right."

> *A meme shattered the imaginary line I had drawn across my Facebook feed.*

These were comments I had seen and had come to expect, while navigating the hate group sewers. I never expected it to show up on my "real social media" with similar comments made by people I knew from real life.

I knew this man and I held different political leanings. I knew he followed a very orthodox Christian dogma. We had, until this point, agreed to disagree about spiritual belief structures. And, until this meme surface from a pit of hate onto my feed, I enjoyed our respectful discourse on the topics of our day.

"----, why are you sharing a meme circulated on hate groups?"

Yep, I started the conversation wrong. He got defensive. I pressed with questions I had been biting my tongue to ask of the people in those groups. Just like in those groups, the likes on his post went down to two. He unfriended and blocked me.

We all know someone who has decided it is easier to blame others for a problem instead of doing the hard work required to fix the problem.

If we all know people who are ready to believe this lie of scapegoating someone else, then we all need to do what we can to show these scared, hurting people that there is a better way to solve the problems facing us.

Takeaway #6

Doing nothing is a way to help the bullies hurt people.

Every small act you do with compassion will move us all towards a more kind and just society. The information in the next chapter will get you started.

Chapter 2

The 5 Steps for a Healthy Conversation

HAVE YOU EVER been in a conversation that went terribly wrong? Everything was going well, and then left turn into a painful train wreck of, "What the heck just happened?" When you replay the conversation in your head, do the parts "I should have said this." and "Where did that come from?" vie for prominence? Does this happen with many people in your life or just a few?

Speaking and acquiring language is a natural skill humans develop. This drive to communicate is also a natural component of being human. But just because we have words and language doesn't mean we are using those tools of words and language to effectively express what we want to say, nor get the response we want.

Before you swear off humanity or resign yourself to the pain being perpetually misunderstood, please keep reading.

While the drive to communicate is naturally acquired, the process of effectively doing so is a learned behavior shared in and passed along through families. If your family shared ineffective tools with you, welcome to the club of adulthood.

Healthy communication is a five-part process. If you skip or ignore a part, problems arise. Conversations turn sideways and veer into painful arguments when these steps are not followed. These five steps for healthy conversations are simple to understand, but will take practice before this skill is reliably integrated into your regular daily use. Take it one conversation at a time. Start with the most difficult.

Why the most difficult? Because that is the conversation which least follows the flow presented below. You could also check to see how your easiest conversations match the healthy flow.

5 Steps of
Healthy Conversations

1. Observation
2. Feelings
3. Needs
4. Requests
5. Backup Plan

Basics of Healthy Communication

Healthy communication is needed to complete the Offensive Compassion Action Recipes offered in Chapter 5. If this chapter is the first time you are seeing this concept, the information may seem daunting. It's okay to be overwhelmed. You do not need to become an expert with healthy communication before combating the hate in this world by spreading love. It does help, and the more closely you follow the five steps of a healthy conversation, the easier and more fun and effective the Offensive Compassion Action Recipes will be for you.

These steps are based on Marshall B. Rosenberg's book, *Non-Violent Communication*, published in 2003. His process has only four steps. Over the years assisting people raised in homes where communication was a weapon, I have found adding a fifth step assures the conversation flows and everyone has their needs met. This information is provided as an introduction to the topic. Much more information is available on the website.

Objective Observations: Look at the world around you and see what is happening without judging what is going on, and without projecting what you think will happen in the future onto this moment. Just report what you take in through your five senses.

Feelings: Take the 1 – 2 seconds needed to acknowledge the feelings inside you which have been triggered by what is going on around you. Don't judge your feeling or blame someone else for you feeling them. These are yours. You can be feeling more than one at a time. Feelings tell you something is important.

> *Every feeling you have is valid, and there is a healthy way to express all of them – even the scary ones.*

Needs: Those feelings popped up because of a need wiggling around inside of you. Based on your experience of similar observations in the past, your brain has already concluded something will happen, and wants something right now to successfully maintain your existence. Everything is life or death for your brain. Label which need is demanding to be met/fixed/helped. The more you ignore the needs, the more pain your brain applies to get you to fill this need. If you can't fill it yourself, you will need help from others.

Requests: With word, ask the other person to do a specific task designed to help you meet this need you just realized you have. Your question is a request, because if the other person refuses to help, or cannot help as you want them to, you must figure out how to fill your need without their assistance or by yourself. Yes, you can. It may not be easy to do, but you can fill your own needs. Request also means, you don't punish the other person for not helping you. Punishment for non-compliance is a demand. To assure your statement is a request and not a demand, assume the other person is unable to help you before you make the request. Pessimistic, yes, but necessary if you grew up under an environment where words were used as weapons instead of to nurture and support.

Backup Plan: Decide how you will help yourself if they do not help you. Then take those actions needed to fulfill your own needs. Unmet needs create pain. The pain will remain until the need your feelings are telling you about is met. Ignoring this innate need will not make it go away.

Try using these steps with the next person you speak too. Or replay the last conversation in your head, and run through what you wish you would have said using these steps. Replaying the bad conversations using this healthy process will validate how these steps could have helped in that situation. It can also make the memory easier, and give you practice in using this skill.

Growing up, words were weapons in my home. The concept of compassion was difficult at first let alone trusting this process enough to follow these steps for healthy communication. The process worked when I used it, so I was determined to use it more often. The concept was so outside of my reality, I needed to write a cheat sheet of more than the suggested "Observe, Feel, Want, Request, Backup Plan". I wrote all of the information from following list on an index card. It will fit if you write small enough. I referred to my cheat sheet so frequently, my index card got smooth and soft. I went through three more cards before this skill felt authentic. Luckily, these steps worked long before I made it through the steps without the cheat sheet.

How to Have a Healthy Conversation

Conversations go awry when we, or the person we are talking to, stray from this basic structure presented below. Look back on all the conversations that did not go well in your past, and you find that one of you left this simple process for some reason.

1. I See/Hear/Touch/Taste/Smell (insert a specific thing).
2. And I feel Love/Joy/Surprise/Anger/Sadness/Fear.
3. Because I need…
    a. Connection
    b. Physical Well-Being
    c. Honesty
    d. Play
    e. Peace
    f. Autonomy
    g. Meaning
4. Will you please (insert action here)?
5. If they say no. I will help myself by…

When in pain, people veer away from the healthy pattern for conversations which causes even more pain. I still refer to my cheat sheet when getting ready for a difficult meeting.

These steps are on my business cards, so palming the card during trying conversations is much less notable. Another great side effect of putting these steps on my business cars is I can share them with other people who also want to create and sustain a life they want to live. Try it yourself. Write the steps on an index card, and you can carry them around with you. Or download the cheat sheet for yourself at our website www.offensive-compassion.com.

Chapter 3

Recognize and Dismantle Blocking Techniques

Ways to Block Healthy Communication

ANTHROPOLOGIST BELIEVE LANGUAGES were created to keep information inside a specific family or social group. If that is true, language was built to express ourselves inside our groups but to block information transfer between groups. Even if you don't use overt controlling tactics such as yelling, there are many other ways we block communication from taking place.

> **Watch Your Step**
>
> Blocking techniques are used by people who are afraid. Providing safety for these people will help to dismantle the technique.

We have all been in conversations that went completely sideways. At the time, trapped on that roller coaster of surprise, you might not have realized what was happening as it unfolded. Only after getting some distance from the person or topic, you can reflect on the conversation and point out where something "went wrong". Below is a list of the most common techniques people use to block communication.

As you read this section, you will recognize examples from your own communication patterns and those of others. This will happen, and you may feel shame. When that happens, keep going.

Before picking up a copy of this book, you were using the tools the way you were trained to use them. You thought you were using them as effectively as humanly possible. Take a moment to grieve the memory when it comes up. Then read on about a better way to make yourself understood. You can start to use this tool for communicating more effectively no matter how many times you messed up in the past.

When you recognize any of the following techniques in a conversation, congratulate yourself for learning and recognizing the attempt to use unhelpful communication tactics. People use these blocking techniques deflect the conversation and avoid the topic.

Mind Reading. Assuming to know what the other person feels and thinks without asking.

> "I know. You're going to tell me…"
> "I've heard this before."
> "Let me guess…"
> "Not again!"

Rehearsing. Planning the response to a statement while missing the statement being said.

> *Most seen is social situation where strangers interact.*
> Person 1: "Nice to meet you. How are you?"
> Person 2: "Nice to meet you, too. I'm fine. How are you?"
> Person 1: "Great. How are you?"

Judging. Evaluating the other person by labeling the comments and/or the person as Good or Bad.

> "They deserved it."
> "Suit them right. What did they expect to happen?"
> "It shouldn't have happened to such nice people."

Name Calling. Referring to another person with a derogatory designation or description to invalidate their experience and or ideas.

> "Stupid."
> "Nazi."
> "Snowflake."
> "Bad people."
> "Millennial."
> "Baby Boomer."
> "Generation X."

Criticism. Expressing your disapproval of someone or something based on perceived faults or mistakes.

> "Should have…"
> "Wouldn't have happened if…"
> "They were too…"

Comparisons. Looking at what happened in other situations where this person or topic was discussed and using the past or future events to pass judgement on the other person.

> "Yes, but _____ did _____, and _____."
> "Don't complain. _____, had a worse time."
> "_____ did it better."
> "Sure mine was terrible, but many people have it worse than I did."

Daydreaming. Getting caught in memories or fantasies while someone is talking to you.

> *That far-off dullness in the other person's expression.*
> Person 1: "What do you think?"
> Person 2: "What?"

> *Daydreaming can be a symptom of abuse or a medical emergency.*

Advising. Looking for an opportunity to tell someone what to do to fix the problem as you see it instead of listening to the person explain their experience.

>Person 1: "Then I turned around, and the door was locked! I was--"
>Person 2: "Did you call a locksmith?"

>Person 1: "It's so bright outside today."
>Person 2: "I have sunscreen if you need it."

Sparring. Invalidating the other person's experience by arguing and debating.

>Person 1: "It's such a nice day."
>Person 2: "It's only a nice day because of global warming."

>Person 1: "Look! There are donuts in the kitchen."
>Person 2: "Those are so bad for you."

Being right. Resisting or ignoring the experiences of others if they do not match your own experiences.

>Person 1: "It's such a nice day."
>Person 2: "No. It is way too bright outside."

>Person 1: "I like _____."
>Person 2: "If you can't name (extreme detail of topic), you don't."

Derailing. Changing the subject as soon as you hear anything that bothers or threatens you.

>Person 1: "Honey, we need to talk."
>Person 2: "Did you see this cat picture?"

>Person 1: "Alright. Enough stalling. Time for bed."
>Person 2: "I'm thirsty."

Threatening. Intentionally expressing yourself in a hostile way to create physical dominance over someone else or to cause the other person to feel as though they are in physical danger.

>Crowding personal space.
>Throwing things or slamming items against surfaces.
>Promising physical, financial or social harm for non-compliance.
>"I will get you fired."
>"You'll never work in this town again."
>"If you tell, I'll deny it."
>"Your family is dead."
>"You'll never see your kids again."
>"No one will believe you."
>"… or else."

> *No one has the right to threaten you. If someone does, they see you as an easy target for their hate. They are wrong.*

Demanding. Stating what you want in a way which does not allow the other person to refuse to help you. Punishment for non-compliance to your desires.

"Clean your room, or you can't go out to play."
"If you really loved me you would…"

Person 1: Can you get me a water, since you are in the kitchen?
Person 2: My hands are full. Wait a sec.
Person 1: I'm going to delete your show if you forget.

Denial of Responsibility. Refusing to acknowledge a possible connection between your actions and your role in the current problem.

"It's not my fault."
"I broke it, but it wasn't my fault."
"I was there, but I didn't call them that. _____, said it."
"I didn't have time."
"I forgot."
"I didn't do it."

Exaggerations. Making outlandish statements about a situation or event being worse or better than it actually is or was to invalidate the other person's experience.

"He always…"
"She never…"

Placating. Agreeing to another person's view point without expressing your own views or experience.

"Yes dear."
"Whatever."
"Yep."

Ignoring. Refuse to take notice of or acknowledge; intentionally disregard for the contributions or comments of another person.

Not responding to comments made by someone.
Not answering questions, and pretending they were never asked.
Pretending not to see the other person.

Dismantling These Blocking Techniques

These techniques work to block communication. Using these techniques is an indication of a problem. Luckily, there are effective methods to get around people using these techniques, and get to the core of the problem between you. Not everyone is ready to solve their problems or wants their problems fixed. Many people are content in their pain.

> *Watch Your Step*
>
> It is not your responsibility to fix someone else's problems or feelings.

It is not your responsibility to fix someone else's problems or feelings. If you choose to communicate with someone, you only agree to listen to their point of view. You do not need to agree with the content of what they are expressing, nor do you need to convince them of something.

Reflective listening is a communication strategy involving two key steps: seeking to understand a speaker's idea, then offering the idea back to the speaker, to confirm the idea has been understood correctly by the listener. Everyone has their own filter when listening to things. Using reflective listening, you can show that you are trying to understand the other person when you notice the conversation going sideways.

Before a misunderstanding, there is point where the conversations or expectations did not align. When you notice a conversation taking a turn or a miscommunication happening, use this technique to get back onto common ground. Use of any blocking technique is an example of the communication going off track.

Find Common Ground with Reflective Listening

There is a way to find common ground when you discover there is a disconnect between what you and the person you are speaking with. Reflective listening is an easy skill to learn and is effective when used to communicate with people who want to talk. Recognizing the disconnect can take a few moments. Allow yourself that time. You will get faster at recognizing the conversation veering away from the natural steps for a healthy conversation presented above with practice. Once you do recognize the turn, use reflective listening to figure out where your companion and yourself disagree.

Steps for Reflective Listening

1. You notice there is a disconnect between what you are hearing and what the other person thinks they are saying.
2. State you need. "Excuse me. I believe I heard that wrong. Can you repeat that?"
3. Person repeats it.
4. You interpret the statement, and restate it as you understand it.
5. Then ask, "Is that right?"
6. Person responds in the affirmative or negative.
7. Work with the person to understand their point of view by repeating steps 4 through 6 as needed.
8. If multiple passes through steps 4 through 6 have occurred with no progress in understanding, you must decide if this is a conversation.

Using the process of reflective listening, you will be able to understand what the other person is trying to convey. You can still disagree with what the person is saying, but at least now the person you are talking to feels heard. Once your conversation companion feels heard, they are usually more open to listening to what you have to say.

As you find opportunities to try this technique to understand people, you many find some people twist what they are arguing about while you are looking for clarification. You are not crazy. Your attempts to communicate are being blocked. Point out the disconnect or change. You might notice some feelings of irritation or hostility in yourself. You also might realize it is the same person or people doing this.

Go through three rounds of listening, reflecting back what the speaker said, and asking for clarification. If no forward progress has been made towards understanding in those three rounds, you might be engaging in a one-sided argument. If the other person is not responding to your attempts at understanding them, or their stance has changed and is now opposite to what it was, you are in an argument. You do not need to argue with anyone. You are under no obligation to remain in this argument. You can stop speaking to them.

> *You are not obligated to argue with anyone, even if they are arguing with you.*

Your silence does not mean this other person "won" or "is right". Your silence means you are done wasting your energy attempting to help someone work through their pain when they are clearly attached to it. If you want to, you can try again later.

Summarizing and paraphrasing are different techniques beginners learning reflective listening skills routinely confuse. Both summarizing and paraphrasing represent the listener attempting to share the speaker's main points as understood by the listener. Summarizing presents this information using the speaker's own words and statements. Paraphrasing presents this information using the listener's words.

When the listener uses their own words to reflect back what the speaker is saying, it means the listener has digested the information. We each have our own personal filters built from personal experience. Different experiences create different filters we perceive the world through. Using your own words to offer a summary of what you believe you heard will clarify what is being shared, and true understanding can take place.

> ### Watch Your Step
> **Just because people say they want to talk, doesn't mean they are willing to reach a consensus.**

Not everyone wants to communicate. If you find yourself needing to engage in reflective listening repeatedly with the same person, that person is not willing to communicate in a healthy manner. They have a reason for wanting to dominate the conversation and/or hurt someone. You must decide if you are able to continue.

Not everyone is healthy enough to communicate with or able to engage in healthy communication. Once you identify a person who is unable or unwilling to engage in a healthy manner, you can end the conversation. You do not owe the other person a conversation, just as they do not owe you a conversation.

Making the decision to stop engaging in an unhealthy conversation is not selfish. When you stop doing things that hurt you, you are setting healthy boundaries.

Settling limits on how many hurtful comments or behaviors you will expose yourself to is a major step in taking real action. It is an action which sets a positive example for others.

People accustomed to treating you and others poorly will offer the most resistance to the new skills you are using. The next chapter shows you what you can expect from others during this transition.

CHAPTER 4

Stages of Grief, Learning and Change

Volumes of information are available on these three concepts. Millions of people have dedicated their lives to uncovering the nuances of each concept and the process humans use to get through them successfully. You don't need to read any of that available information before using Offensive Compassion to make your life and relationships better. You do need to know that learning, change, and grief are part of everyone's life.

Grief, learning and change affect everyone's ability to communicate and interact in the world depending on which stage they are in.

> *Grief is how well we have learned to live with the change.*

Everything you learn creates a change.

Every choice is a change.

Every change causes grief.

If you want the change facing you, your progress through the process of grief will be quick. If you do not want the change, you progress slowly, or even get stuck in one of the stages of grief. When we don't want a change, but are forced to accept this new reality, we must learn to function in a world where this new version of our life continues. Grief is how well we have learned to live with the change. How well you have learned something is called competency.

The table below shows how people use strikingly similar steps to successfully navigate the experiences of grief, learning and change.

STAGES OF:	GRIEF	LEARNING	CHANGE
1	Denial	Novice	Precontemplation
2	Anger	Advanced Beginner	Contemplation
3	Bargaining	Competent	Preparation
4	Depression	Proficient	Action
5	Acceptance (and Relapse)	Expert (Maintenance)	Maintenance (and Relapse)

Every change launches us into the natural process of grief. Even the good things we want in our lives send us through the process momentarily as our mind learns to live with this new fact. Check out the similarities of each stage on the next few pages. Where someone is during these stages affect how they are able to communicate with us. Again, it is not your responsibility to fix anyone or rescue them from themselves. This information is presented to help you understand where people are and how best to reach them when going out into the world with Offensive Compassion.

Stage 1

The first stage is where we all start. This stage of grief, learning or change is about not knowing, and not being able to clearly see what is going on.

Grief calls it **Denial**. Denial is a way to keep functioning in the world by cutting off emotions, and becoming numb to the world. Denial protects us by only letting the information we can handle into our brain. Ignoring the pain of the change and functioning is the name of this game.

Learning calls it *Novice*. A novice doesn't even know what they don't know. They have a general concept of the topic, but no ability to put this general concept into actionable steps. This is where we all start learning by following steps someone else has given us.

Change calls it **Precontemplation**. People in this stage are not even thinking about changing something. They don't see their behaviors or actions as a problem in their lives, or they are resigned to the pain of their actions and behaviors believing they have no ability to change their current state.

This first stage of grief, learning or change is the start of understanding. Once a bit of understanding creeps into our minds, we travel into the second stage of these processes.

Stage 2

The second stage of grief, learning or change is where we start to understand there is a lot we don't know. Not knowing stuff mean we understand there is something important out there that we do not have. This is a very frustrating stage.

Grief calls it **Anger**. Anger is getting mad at the person or situation, and even yourself for the trauma which occurred. The target of your anger may be an innocent bystander. This is your brain trying to fight its way out of the pain. Fight, Flight, or Freeze – works with a physical attack, so your body uses it for an emotional attack of grief, too.

Learning calls it *Advanced Beginner*. An advance beginner is someone with just barely acceptable performance level after gaining experience coping with real life experiences. The real life application of the topic shows the person the huge gaps in their understanding and abilities. More practice is the only thing that gets people through this stage.

<u>Change</u> calls it <u>Contemplation</u>. People are more and more aware of the potential benefits of making a change during the contemplation stage, but as they think about the benefits, they can also see how much effort this new thing could take if they commit to it. Change is uncertainty.

People don't like uncertainty. Many people view change as a process of giving up something they know rather than a process to gain something more useful than their old tools.

The second stage of grief, learning or change is about realizing there is something else, but you don't have it, and getting it will take effort. Many people get stuck in this stage. Once the person commits to the possibility of more, they progress through this stage.

Stage 3

The third stage of grief, learning or change is about making this route you have chosen as easy as possible for yourself. The person has committed to getting what they realized they didn't have and see the benefits, but they also want it to be an easy acquisition, so we can get through without draining our energies.

Grief calls it **Bargaining**. Bargaining is making deals with the past and future to change the present. If I promise to do (something), then it will make (something else) happen. "If only I did this..." "If this sign happens, then everything will be alright." It's your brain trying to logic its way out of the pain.

Learning calls it *Competent*. – People in this stage have enough personal exposure and working knowledge of many aspects of the skill being learned. They start to understand the big picture, and are starting to question the rules and rigidness of the step in the structure they were using before. They see patterns between situations and adapt what they have learned to these different situations with some success.

Change calls it **Preparation**. The preparation stage is where people start to make small changes to prepare for the bigger changes ahead. Gathering supplies, making lists, talking to experts who know what to expect are all aspects of this preparation state. It is about gathering information to make your next step work.

Stage three of grief, learning or change is about making the journey ahead as easy and quick as possible. Once someone realized they must take action to get the new thing they do not have, they fall into stage four.

Stage 4

The fourth stage of stage of grief, learning or change is the grunt work. It is the hardest leg of the journey because it seems like there is no end.

Grief calls it **Depression**. In this stage of grief, the person starts to realize there is no way to change what happened. As this realization settles over them, questions about the viability of continuing in a world where this has happened come up along with intense sadness. Remember, grief is a change you don't want, and getting through grief is needing to take actions, you don't want to take. Of course, there is a feeling of helplessness. This is a necessary healthy step you need to take to get through grief. It will pass.

Learning calls it *Proficient*. People reach proficiency with a topic when the tools and concepts are internalized, and they can apply this new skill to various situations without agonizing over their actions. Their understanding seems intuitive and holistic.

Change calls it **Action**. This is where people start taking direct action in order to accomplish their goals. Attempts may fail, but the person tries to accomplish something another way. They are figuring out how to make it work, and realize they must do something to find whatever it is that is missing.

Stage four of grief, learning or change is about doing something to reach your goal. Grief is stagnated when people refuse to move towards the new normal after a loss while learning and change are making progress towards what they want to gain.

Stage 5

The fifth stage of grief, learning or change is what people will reach if they keep moving through the hard parts. The final stage is to integrate this new information into your life in a seamless and healthy manner.

Grief calls it **Acceptance**. This stage is about finding the new normal and living with it. It's not "Okay" nor "Alright" that something happened, but the person finds a way to integrate this information into their life in a way to allow them to find joy again, and to live a meaningful life in spite of what happened.

Learning calls it **Expert**. An expert on a topic has fully internalized both the ideas and the actions into their normal existence. Their understanding is intuitive, and they integrate new information quickly figuring out new challenges easily. Things appear to "just work out correctly" for these people. In reality, they are still learning daily, and often seek out experts in other areas to integrate completely separate information into what they have learned about their favorite topic.

<u>**Change**</u> calls it <u>**Maintenance**</u>. Maintenance is about strengthening the new skill or behavior while activity avoiding engaging in the old less useful behaviors. People have integrated the new skill or behavior into their lives and are gaining personal assurances that this new skill or behavior works better than the old one.

> *Watch Your Step*
>
> **New habits, no matter how much more effective they are, take energy to create. Old habits are very attractive when we get tired. Plan for slips.**

When something changes, whether we wanted the change, or we didn't want the change, the old patterns will be strong draws for us. This urge drawing us back into old patterns is called Relapse. These old patterns worked for us in the past. We are very good at them. When a new thing is threatening to take the place of the old favorite pattern, tool, behavior or reality, we go backwards towards the thing we are giving up instead of forward to the new thing.

It happens in grief, learning and change. The lure of our old patterns is hardest to ignore when we are tired or placed in a stressful situation.

Planning how you will get through different stressful situations before they happen is one way to avoid relapse. You can't avoid all of it, though. Plan how to get back on track when you slip back into the old patterns.

Moving Forward through These Processes

I believe each of these process breaks down to a stage of grief. Grief is our method for dealing with change. Some changes we welcome, like learning and friendship. Changes that hurts us are not welcome, like failing at something, a death of a loved one, or the multitude of small disappointments which build up. Each change causes grief. If we welcome the change, this process of grieving is swift. If we didn't want the change, the process can be very painful and slow, as we fight the inevitable truth.

Here's how to tell if you are stuck in a stage of grief.

Are you constantly thinking about something that makes you any other feeling than happy?

If yes, walk through the stages above, and at each stage ask yourself: Where did I do something like this? What did I learn? How will I be better next time?

My favorite questions to push myself through tough spots are:

What are you feeling?

What do you want?

Listen to your answer. It is your truth.

The secret of change is to focus all of your energy not on fighting the old, but on building the new.

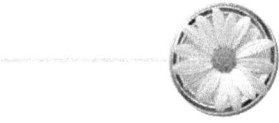

SOCRATES

Chapter 5

Action Recipes

None of the following acts of compassion collected in this book cost money. Instead, they cost time and energy. To invest either of those two resources, you need to prepare yourself. That is why we have started the list of 24 things you can do today to combat hate in the real world with self-care.

It all starts with you. Yes, you are reading this book, so you want actionable steps. But here is the kicker with any of the steps… you can't do them well until you take care of yourself. Taking care of yourself means listening to yourself. Listening to yourself means you will discover what you need to remove the pain which is preventing you from achieving your goals. Removing pain frees up emotional space and energy to live the life you imagine. You can also better recognize pain and the needs in others. Helping people to fill their own needs is another way to create the positive change you want to inspire in the world.

Each Action Recipe offers clear steps to complete the activity, some common reactions you may experience after completing the actions and how to continue after such reactions. Each activity also has a suggested use and a suggested non-use.

Compassion is an active expression. After you have completed an activity, take a moment to review how it went. This will help you integrate the information, and to add your personal flare to the positive change you want in the world.

After each Action Recipe, you will find five questions to help you reflect on the experience, and if you choose to do it again, how to add your own flare.

There is no right way to do compassion. Compassion is a moving target. Do what you can, where you are. When presented with a choice to be kind or cruel, choose kindness. You will find your circle of influence grows the more you practice these techniques on the following pages.

Each of these activities has been taught effectively in a classroom setting and utilized in the real world. Courageous students helped select which activities to include in this book. They also requested the worksheets and trackers they found most useful be included.

Worksheets, trackers and samples of selected Action Recipes are included in Chapter 6. Additional information for each is also provided on the website.

#1 Check to See How You Are Feeling

We are human; therefore, you and I have needs. Those needs are hiding behind our feelings. By disconnecting from these feelings, we are suppressing our innate needs. We can only function for a finite amount of time without having our own needs met before we hurt ourselves and by extension, our loved ones.

We start the path of Offensive Compassion by doing something completely offensive to many unhealthy people, we start by acknowledging our feelings.

There is a well-respected idea in psychology called Maslow's Hierarchy of Needs. Abraham Maslow believed people have a set of motivation systems separate from the, then popular, idea of behaviors motivated only by rewards (like Pavlov and his dogs) or by unconscious desires (like Freud and his obsession with mommy issues). Maslow believed that people are motivated to reach self-actualization, but are blocked from that ultimate life goal when our needs are not met. He believed only after the most basic needs are filled can a person attempt to fill less concrete needs and effectively contribute to the society we live in.

His theory has been modified a bit over the years, but basically it looks like a pyramid with Basic Needs at the bottom, Psychological Needs in the middle, and Self-Fulfillment Needs at the top.

OFFENSIVE COMPASSION

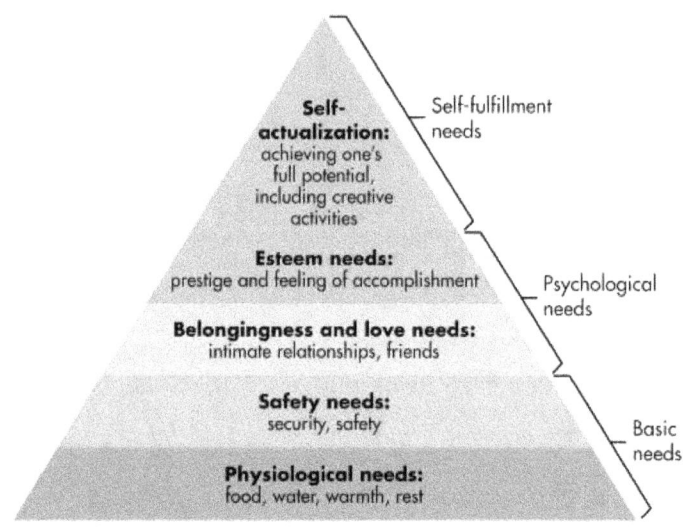

MASLOW'S HIERARCHY OF NEEDS

Prep Time

None.

Action Time

5 – 20 seconds. Quicker with experience.

Steps

1. Pause in your daily life.
2. Ask yourself: How am I feeling?
3. Allow whatever answer comes up.
4. Ask yourself: What do I need right now to feel better?
5. Allow whatever answer comes up to be heard.

The words we use while speaking to ourselves matter. Some people prefer asking what they NEED while others prefer WANT. Try this activity using the two options interchangeably until you discover which word you prefer.

Benefits of Trying this Action

A substantial number of people purposefully disengage from their emotions. This is a survival skill only discovered after many other tools have failed. It is caused by pain. Some emotions hurt. To stop the hurt, we stop the emotions. This technique works for physical injuries like bleeding, so it is natural we try it on emotional injuries.

When you are in a dangerous situation, this skill of cutting off our emotions is a lifesaver. When we are engaging with destructive people, this technique helps us set safe, invisible, personal boundaries. But when we use this survival skill regularly, our emotions become harder and harder to feel, and thus more difficult to figure out what we actually need to keep our survival going beyond the current moment.

Figuring out what we feel, clues us into what we need. Feelings which hurt or drain you mean whatever it is you need is not available in that location. Feelings which feel good or energize you mean you are getting whatever you need in that location. It is important to check on yourself throughout the day to recognize what is happening to you, because our needs change from one moment to the next.

Filling your needs will make it easier for you to help other. If you are not ready to help others, then filling your own needs will make people less irritating to you.

Action Review and Practice

Now it's your turn. Remember, these are skills and tools you can use in your daily life. As with any new skill or tool, you need practice more than once before you get all the steps down. The following questions will assist you to practice and eventually master this skill.

Each time you complete this Action Recipe, take a moment to answer the following questions.

1. When did you use this Action Recipe?

2. What part(s) do you think went well?

3. What part(s) was(were) more difficult than you thought it would be?

4. How can you tweak the action to make the activity easier for you next time?
   (List 2 or 3 ideas)

5. When can you use this Action Recipe in your life?
   (List 2 or 3 ideas)

#2 KNOW YOUR PREFERRED PATTERNS

We play favorites. The secret is playing your favorites consciously. By "favorites", I mean all of our preferences and ways of doing things.

By the time we reach school age, most people have already labeled themselves or been label by people around them as a "morning person", a "night owl", a "social butterfly", or a "wall flower", and various other labels we acquire. We might buy into this assessment, but is it true for you now? This process will help you remove those labels others have given you and discover the natural ebbs and flows of your personal energy patterns. Feel free to substitute: Optimal Performance Patterns for any mention of energy patterns.

Prep Time

Time to grab a few sheets of paper and a writing implement.

Note: This activity is completed most quickly via analog hard copy. Moving to electronic data collection may hamper your execution of this technique.

Action Time

Choose 1: Over the course of 1 Day, 1 Week, and 1 Month.

Steps

1. Grab your paper and pen
2. Across the Top make four columns. Label:
   a) Column 1: Time of Day
   b) Column 2: How much Energy do you have?
   c) Column 3: How are you feeling?
   d) Column 4: What do you need?
3. In the first column labeled, Time of Day, list the hours of the day. You can start at 12:00 AM through 12:00 PM, or Start the first line with the hour you plan to wake up in the morning. Wherever you start, list all 24 hours of the day.
4. Start filling out the tracker.
5. Once an hour, pause for a minute in your day and answer the questions. Using these simple guidelines:
   a) *Amount of Energy:* On a scale of 1 through 7 with 1 being sleeping and 7 being very high energy, note your current energy level.

Sleeping	Very Low Energy	Somewhat Low Energy	Neutral	Somewhat High Energy	High Energy	Very High Energy
1	2	3	4	5	6	7

   b) *Feelings and Emotions:* Note which emotions or feelings are currently present in your mind. You may feel more than one. If you have a larger emotional vocabulary use it. If you are still working on describing your emotions, use these as you discover more ways to describe your mood.

Love	**Joy**	**Surprise**
Anger	**Sadness**	**Fear**

c) *Needs:* If you can think of something missing at that moment, write it down. If you can't think of anything, leave it blank.
6. Once you filled out the notes for your first hour, set a timer for 60 minutes.
7. When the timer goes off in one hour, gather your tracker page and fill in your comments on the next hour.
8. Set your time for one more hour, and continue this process until you go to bed at night.
9. When you wake up, start another tracker, and mark your observations.
10. Once you have completed a 24-hour cycle, look at the pattern your day has created by answering these questions:
    a) When did you wake up?
    b) When did you go to bed?
    c) Which time frame did you have the most energy?
    d) Which time frame did you have the least energy?
    e) What part of your day was the easiest?
    f) Which part of your day was the hardest?

Benefits of Trying this Action

The more cycles you track your behaviors through, the clearer your unique patterns will become. Once you know your innate preferred patterns, you can use them to your advantage. These patterns are a super power you can use to reach any goal, and avoid uncountable pain. High energy hours can be allocated to tasks you need to be high energy for. Move things around in your day to benefit you. If the items cannot be moved, you can come up with strategies to increase your energy to the required level before tackling the activity to make sure you can finish the task successfully.

Common Results

You have just finished tracking your circadian rhythms, the natural ebb and flow of your body's clock. No one is at peak levels of energy 24-hours straight, even people pulling "all-nighters". Humans have an internal 23-hour clock. This hour lag, is felt by all of us. The time of day and how it shows itself is different for everyone. Below are some common findings.

The Mid-Afternoon Slump.
Our bodies send out "sleep signals" at night and mid-afternoon. This time frame is based on how many hours you have been awake, which may explain why we want to grab an afternoon nap. Other factors, like the kinds of food we ate recently, how many hours we've been in one location, how hydrated we are and how packed our schedules are can add to this feeling of low energy.

Look at the things you did before and after this slump to see how you can shift this energy. Plan ahead for tomorrow using the information about low energy to schedule something that works with your natural rhythm.

The Mid-Morning Slump.
This is most likely a sleep hangover. Either you have ignored your body's need for sleep, food, water or any other form of physical comfort (the lowest level of Maslow's Hierarchy of Needs) and now your body is demanding this need be filled.

If this is a regular occurrence, look at the way you fill your basic needs. Can you get to bed 30 minutes earlier at night? Can you prepare a breakfast your body can use, or a snack to revive the energy you need? Are you wearing enough/few enough layers of clothing to maintain a comfortable body temperature? All of these things play a part.

Unexpected Energy Period.

We buy into the labels people give us. But once in a while we have an opportunity to see past those limitations. A period of unexpected energy is just that. You can accomplish more than you thought.

Look at what you were doing before and after this period to see if this boost was due to your natural rhythms, or the people or events around you. Whichever discovery you make, you can use that information to help energize yourself at lower part of your day.

Unexpected Slump Period.

We buy into the labels people give us. But once in a while we have an opportunity to see past those limitations. A period of unexpected low energy is just that.

Look at what you were doing before and after this period to see if this slump was due to your natural rhythms, or the people or events around you. Whichever discovery you make, you can use that information to help schedule your time in the future to avoid difficult activities at this time or put supports in place to increase your energy to the required levels.

Where to Use This

You can use this technique of tracking energy to schedule your day. Such as:

- Scheduling that Root Canal during an energy slump.
- Volunteering to help a friend move for the two hours you have the most energy.
- Suggesting a time you are high energy for when the one person who can get under your skin wants to discuss something.

Where to Avoid Using This

You should refrain from using this technique when taking a moment to track your behavior would be dangerous. Such as:

- While running a marathon.
- While driving down the road.
- While using a sharp knife.

Additional resources for this Action Recipe are provided in Chapter 6 to assist you in creating positive changes in the real world.

Action Review and Practice

Now it's your turn. Remember, these are skills and tools you can use in your daily life. As with any new skill or tool, you need practice more than once before you get all the steps down. The following questions will assist you to practice and eventually master this skill.

Each time you complete this Action Recipe, take a moment to answer the following questions.

1. When did you use this Action Recipe?

2. What part(s) do you think went well?

3. What part(s) was(were) more difficult than you thought it would be?

4. How can you tweak the action to make the activity easier for you next time?
   (List 2 or 3 ideas)

5. When can you use this Action Recipe in your life?
   (List 2 or 3 ideas)

Heroes are never perfect. But they are brave. They're authentic. They're courageous, determined, discreet, and they have grit.

WADE DAVIS

#3 KEEP YOUR SELF PROMISES

Being able to keep the promises you make to yourself is the cornerstone of adulthood. When you trip over to the legal age of 18, you are considered an adult in the eyes of the law, but without being able to keep the promises you make to yourself, you will never pass your own litmus test of adulthood.

Prep Time

The time needed to reflect on your goals and actions.

Action Time

Daily recommitment to your integrity.

Steps

1. Stop making quick promises to yourself.
2. Set SMART Goals to reach the promise by having a specific end point, quantifiable progress, and deadlines.
3. Give yourself a consequence for failure that you don't want to do, and set a reward for success you really do want.
4. Do what you said you were going to do.
5. Acknowledge the effort and skill required of yourself to keep this promise.
6. Celebrate your success with that reward you promised yourself.

Benefits of Trying this Action

We live in different spots on this planet Earth. We have each seen and done things we are not proud of, things we want to take back, or do over in a better way. We have all let ourselves down – in the past. We have let others down – in the past. And in the future, it will happen again, and again until we strengthen that habit of keeping our promises.

It is never too late to start over in a better direction towards your goals. Learning how to keep your promises to yourself, and building the skills of keeping promises you make to yourself, will restore your hope in the future. It will give you confidence in yourself. You will learn to trust again.

If you are disillusioned by experiences in your past, and heard 1,001 excuses in your head to skip this section, you can do this, too. Start small.

Common Results

Start Small.

The internet is full of 7-Day and 30-Day Challenges. This is the practicing tool people are using to strengthen this skill of keeping self-promises. But seven days is a long commitment for someone who has lost faith in themselves. Start by promising yourself you will finish reading this paragraph.

You did it!

Great job keeping that promise you yourself. Now look for a promise which required a little more time investment, like take three deep breaths before falling asleep tonight.

You keep your promises to others, but not to yourself.

This means you have the skills required to keep promises, but you did not have the motivation in the past to keep promises without the threat of pain failing others causes you. Ask yourself what is the most painful part of breaking your promise to someone else? What are you getting or maintaining by breaking your promise to yourself?

These are difficult questions, because you are fighting your brain, your arch nemesis and greatest defender rolled up in one convenient package which never leaves you alone. You must convince your brain that these changes you are promising yourself will not kill you.

Small promises are easy.

It's the big ones that are hard. Words are words. It is the meaning and energy we attach to them which makes them feel bigger, harder... more or less anything. Once you come to the point where you realize small promises are easy to keep, you are ready to accomplish everything you set your mind to.

The secret is to break the "big promises" into a series of "small promises". Just as you would break a big goal into smaller sized goals, you need to do the same with your promises. Then, baby-step your way to the goal. This is a way to move yourself past resistance and trick your brain into feeling safe while you push your personal envelope.

Where You Can Use This

You can use this technique of keeping promises to yourself in everyday life such as:
- Getting ready for bed when you said you would.
- Sitting down to pay your bills.
- Doing household chores.

Where to Avoid Using This

You should refrain from keeping promises to yourself if they are camouflaged way of punishing yourself. Such as:
- Not eating when you are hungry.
- Staying up late and finishing some task even though being this late will make tomorrow all the more difficult.
- Making a promise you don't want to keep, and then using this instance of not keeping promises as proof you are unworthy or incapable of attaining your larger goals.

Action Review and Practice

Now it's your turn. Remember, these are skills and tools you can use in your daily life. As with any new skill or tool, you need practice more than once before you get all the steps down. The following questions will assist you to practice and eventually master this skill.

Each time you complete this Action Recipe, take a moment to answer the following questions.

1. When did you use this Action Recipe?

2. What part(s) do you think went well?

3. What part(s) was(were) more difficult than you thought it would be?

4. How can you tweak the action to make the activity easier for you next time?
   (List 2 or 3 ideas)

5. When can you use this Action Recipe in your life?
   (List 2 or 3 ideas)

Be kinder to yourself,
and then let your kindness
flood the world.

PEMA CHODRÖN

#4   Do Something You Enjoy

> *Joy is a feeling which by definition energizes you, invigorates you, and is something you look forward to engaging in. The challenge here is to do something you enjoy, by yourself. Experience joy by yourself means you can feel this inspiring energy without waiting or relying on another person or thing to bring you happiness.*

This is a book about Offensive Compassion. There is nothing more offensive to unhappy people than a person knows themselves well enough to know what brings them joy and has the courage and self-respect to feel that joy when and how they want to feel it.

Prep Time

Time required to find paper and a writing implement.

Action Time

15 – 30 minutes to make the list. Then 5 minutes to 60 minutes to complete something you enjoy.

Steps

1. Gather some paper and a pen.
2. Number the lines on the page 1 through 10.

3. List 10 or more enjoyable activities which bring you joy or may bring you joy if you did them now.
4. Estimate how long it would take you to complete one of these enjoyable things. Listen you your favorite song. Find your favorite color / smell / animal in the world.
5. Write down how long you would need to enjoy this item beside each item.
6. Experience one item on your list of enjoyable things.
7. Allow yourself to enjoy the experience.

Benefits of Trying this Action

The hardest thing to do in hard times, is to do something soft. Being kind to yourself, and reminding yourself of the good things in the world you are fighting for, go a long way in helping us get through whatever is in front of us. Doing something for your enjoyment is a kind thing to do to yourself and a reminder to others that there is something still worthwhile in this world.

Common Results

Over Indulgence Remorse.

The current culture in the USA demands consumerism and celebrity worship, but the act of actually enjoying ourselves has been taken way. Americans are bombarded with the idea that more is better. This is not true, especially with things we enjoy. Our free time is so sparse and inconsistent, we pack these precious moments with as much enjoyment as we possibly can, to fill up for the lean times coming. This mind set turns the enjoyable fun into a stressful task to get through. Stop it.

Take five minutes out of your day to do something just for you, and only you. If you find yourself so over scheduled the idea of another item for your to-do list creates heart palpitations, breathe. These enjoyable minutes can be short moments. Start small. Commit to doing one small things every day. Use the favorite dishes, wear your favorite color, or sing your favorite song while doing something miserable. Enjoyment does not have to be a big event. Slip it into a choice you are already making.

Hurried Through Activity.

There are many reasons to hurry through an activity you enjoy. Not many of them are good reasons, because part of the enjoyment is engaging at your own pace. If you are having difficulty even starting something fun, hurrying through the item seems like a great way to squeeze it into your day. Slow down. Notice the world around you as you experience this fun. What does the ground feel like? Are you holding something? How heavy is it? Are you warm or cold? What can you smell? What can you hear? Listen for the small sounds behind the noise. This is your life. This is your time, use it to recharge yourself. You deserve it.

Criticized for Enjoying Yourself.

First, activities are not enjoyable nor recharging when the act hurts someone. Enjoying a cup of coffee is not hurting anyone. But some people will criticize you for enjoying it. Let's face it, misery loves company, and unhappy people do not like to see others enjoying themselves. If you get criticized for enjoying yourself, you have just received valuable information, not about yourself, but about the person criticizing you. Whatever they are complaining about it what they need more of in their lives. Control, not feeling alone in their pain, autonomy, money or healthy energy. Did the person just lament about the life of people on a stereotypical coffee plantation? Or the lack of a living wage for your barista? The overall complaint cannot be rectified right now, so what is the point of the person complaining? They want you to join them in their unhappiness.

Don't engage with them.

You are not doing this for them. You are finding enjoyment and happiness in the moment for yourself. You are recharging yourself. You owe them nothing. Take your moment of fun.

Strangers Join In.

Believe it or not, having fun and enjoying yourself in public creates an island of inclusion. Even sitting somewhere quietly reading, you will discover people congregate around those having fun. This is because humans are social creatures, even if you don't want to be, others do. We can tell when someone is having fun. We want to join the fun. Given any sign of acceptance, we will join the group having fun. It is a very old survival tactic honed long before agriculture and cities. Don't change your fun, but let others join in and experience the island of compassion and joy your activity creates. This is Offensive Compassion.

Where You Can Use This

You can use this technique of inserting enjoyable activities into your day with any item on your to-do list. Such as:
- Eating a meal.
- Checking the daily mail.
- Getting dressed for the day.

Where to Avoid Using This

You should refrain from using this technique if inserting an enjoyable activity into your day if doing so would hurt you or someone else. Such as:
- During a hostage situation.
- While leaving a burning building.
- Attempting a water rescue.

Additional resources for this Action Recipe are provided in Chapter 6 to assist you in creating positive changes in the real world.

Action Review and Practice

Now it's your turn. Remember, these are skills and tools you can use in your daily life. As with any new skill or tool, you need practice more than once before you get all the steps down. The following questions will assist you to practice and eventually master this skill.

Each time you complete this Action Recipe, take a moment to answer the following questions.

1. When did you use this Action Recipe?

2. What part(s) do you think went well?

3. What part(s) was(were) more difficult than you thought it would be?

4. How can you tweak the action to make the activity easier for you next time?
   (List 2 or 3 ideas)

5. When can you use this Action Recipe in your life?
   (List 2 or 3 ideas)

#5 Reduce Your Irritations

Small irritations cumulate into large distractions without conscience thought. There could be hundreds of small unneeded annoyances in your life adding to your stress and difficulty doing what you want to do. Removing these unnecessary hurts in our lives opens us to the possibility of responding to others with more patience and understanding.

Prep Time

15 minutes to discover some of the invisible items in your space.

Action Time

5 minutes – 1 hour per item found.

Steps

1. Set a timer for 10 minutes
2. Gather some paper and pen.
3. Look around your current environment.
4. Notice the items around you and ask yourself why these items are here.
5. What about your space drains your energy, causes you stress, irritation, or sadness?
6. List those items on the paper.
7. List all items which come up until the timer goes off.

    a. Allow every item you discover a space on your list without censuring it. You were actively ignoring the needs these items represent a few moments ago. You don't hate these items, you dislike what they represent.

    b. Weird stuff will fall onto this list. Allow it.

8. After the timer goes off, stop adding to the list. Put the list down and walk away from the list for a couple minutes.

9. Next, go back to the list and look at the items you listed. (You can add the two of three items vexing you during the separation time.)

10. Separate these items into the general categories of:

    a. Physical Environment
    b. Health
    c. Finances
    d. Family/Relationships
    e. Learning
    f. Spirit
    g. Contribution

11. You will notice one category has accumulated more items than the others. This is the area of your life where you have the most unmet needs right now.

12. Pick one "simple" item from the list and fix it.

13. Try to fix one or more items a day until the items on the list no longer irritate you.

Benefits of Trying This Action

Attention is a strange thing. What we focus on increase, while what you don't focus on fades away. This fading does not mean the item is gone. Instead, it means we are exerting energy to see something else. If you are in a dangerous situation, surrounded by toxic people cutting you down at every pass, this is a well-honed skill. And if you are in a safe place surrounded by love and comfort, this ability to ignore things is still at work. It preserves our sanity and ability to function in the world regardless of what we "see" around us. Improving one area will slowly improve all the areas, and help create the life you want to be living.

Physical Environment.

This category holds everything which has physical space in your life. The inanimate objects you surround yourself with. Your home, possessions, and the space you find yourself in right now.

Health.

This category holds items related to your body's function. Fitness, allergies, major medical conditions, and small passing maladies all go in here.

Finances.

This category holds all of your monetary concerns. Employment, self-employment, bank accounts, savings, bills, retirement plans, and anything else related to your ability to provide for yourself and loved ones goes here.

Family/Relationships.

Let's face it, people can be irritating, too. This category is for the relationships you have in your life. Family, friends, loves, and enemies. If you are sharing your life with someone, irritations arise, not because you dislike them, but because you dislike something their actions represent to you. If you don't share your life with someone else, there is a different set of irritations nagging at you. Again, these are needs you have which are not being met.

Learning.

As a species, humans are inquisitive creatures. This is the category to hold all the items related to learning a skill, perfecting a talent, or starting something new. You have these needs even if you are not perusing a formal education. Watching a DIY show on television about home improvement or a YouTube video on videogame techniques fall into this category, because you are being intellectually curious.

Spirit.

This category is for those items related to your spiritual side. Regardless of your religious leaning, you have a need to be connected to something greater than yourself. While irritations arising from sharing your spiritual beliefs with a group of people would fall into relationships, this category is for your relationship with yourself and your ideals.

Contribution.

We want to add something of value to the world around us. This category is how we are doing that. Contribution is your legacy, volunteering, helping others, and the positive impact you want to make on this world. You are reading this book, so you want to make an impact.

Doing this exercise may expose some uncomfortable truths. I know it did the first time I tried it. Clearing away your irritations is a way to see and fill your needs. Once your needs are satisfied, you are more able to be kind and compassionate in the world.

Where You Can Use This

You can use this technique of itemizing your irritations to figure out where your emotional and physical energies are being sapped. Such as:
- Not wanting to go home.
- Snapping at strangers on the street.
- Contemplating a car accident.

Where to Avoid Using This

You should refrain from using this technique when writing something down is not advisable. Such as:
- Standing behind someone at the ATM
- Swimming in the open ocean
- Driving down the Autobahn

Additional resources for this Action Recipe are provided in Chapter 6 to assist you in creating positive changes in the real world.

Action Review and Practice

Now it's your turn. Remember, these are skills and tools you can use in your daily life. As with any new skill or tool, you need practice more than once before you get all the steps down. The following questions will assist you to practice and eventually master this skill.

Each time you complete this Action Recipe, take a moment to answer the following questions.

1. When did you use this Action Recipe?

2. What part(s) do you think went well?

3. What part(s) was(were) more difficult than you thought it would be?

4. How can you tweak the action to make the activity easier for you next time?
   (List 2 or 3 ideas)

5. When can you use this Action Recipe in your life?
   (List 2 or 3 ideas)

#6 Use Positive Descriptions

State things in an affirmative manner. Say what you want to happen instead of what you don't want to happen.

Prep Time

None.

Action Time

10 seconds to come up with a better way to state something.

Steps

1. Think about what you are going to say.
2. If you plan to use a negative statement, swap it with a positive one.
3. When you trip up and say what you don't want instead of staying what you do want, restate the comment in a manner more in line with what you want instead of what you don't want.
4. Allow yourself you learn.

Stating things in a positive way does not mean you are spouting rainbows and glitter every time you speak. That would be ill advised. When you shift to stating things in the positive, it means you are moving your attention to what you do want to happen instead of warning against what you do not want to happen. Here are some examples of the difference.

Focuses on what you DON'T want:		Focuses on what you DO want:
"Don't get hurt."	vs.	"Have fun."
"I can't be late for this."	vs.	"I want to be on time for this."
"I can't afford that."	vs.	"I'm using my money on something more important right now."
"I can't get sick right now."	vs.	"I'm going to stay healthy.
"Sorry, I'm not going to your party."	vs.	"I have a previous commitment that day. I hope you have a great time."
"Don't go over there."	vs.	"Stay here."

Benefits if Trying this Action

Using positive language with yourself and with others reduces conflict, by clearly stating what we went instead of what we are trying to avoid. This straight forwardness subverts innate defensiveness in others. It might seem hokey and fake the first few times you use this new method of communicating. Keep at it. You'll be surprised to see the overall improvements to your mood and ability to express yourself with people.

Common Results

Mood Boost.

Negative statements quietly cut us down with a million silent attacks. When we speak negatively to ourselves, we undermine our ability to accomplish things we want, because we are focusing on all the obstacles in front of what we want. Using positive ways of expressing the same concerns, reduces those invisible blows and gives us more emotional energy to face the day.

Weird look from others, then a smile.

Very descriptive, yes. When you state something positively after you have been in the habit of stating things negatively, you are changing your patterns of interaction. This will cause the people who know your old patterns to look at you strangely for a moment. Some of the people around you will look at you strangely and after a moment smile. Many will jump right to the smile. These people who smile are your easy allies on the path to healthy communication and spreading compassion. You might be surprised by which of your friends, family and colleges fall into these categories.

Weird look from others, then a frown.

When you state something positively when you have been in the habit of stating things negatively, you are changing your patterns of interaction. This will cause other people to look at you strangely for a moment. People who look at you strangely, then frown or attack your new pattern are threatened by your new autotomy. These are the people who will be most resistant to your expressions of healthy communication and compassion.

If you are dealing with very unhealthy people, they may even lash out at you with an instant put down or insult. Their response has nothing to do with your comment and everything to do with their fear. Your new pattern of being kind to yourself has pointed out how cruel they are to themselves. They want company in their misery. You don't owe them company in misery. If cornered and forced to respond to their irrationality, I offer my go to response, "Thanks."

Things start to go smoothly.

One of the most surprising side effects of learning how to state what you want instead of what you are trying to avoid, is that things start to go right. What you focus on happens more often than what you do not focus on. Therefore, focusing on what you are trying to accomplish instead of what you are trying to avoid makes what you want to accomplish happen more often.

Where You Can Use This

You can use this technique of stating things in a positive manner any time you are expressing an opinion or desire. Such as:
- Choosing a dinner location.
- Selecting clothing for the day.
- Discussing a building project.
- Talking to yourself.

Where to Avoid Using This

You should refrain from using this technique of stating things positively when someone's safety is at stake. Such as:
- Halting someone from touching down power lines. "Don't come over here."
- Setting rules about touching hot stovetops. "Don't touch the hot stove."
- When you see a big bug on someone. "Don't move."

Each of these items CAN be stated in the positive. If there is an emergency and you can't think of them in the split second needed to take action, toss the positive statement and take action.

Positive alternatives for the statements above could be:
- Power Lines Down – "Stay away"
- Dangerous Area – "Keep back"
- Scary Lifeform – "Freeze"

Action Review and Practice

Now it's your turn. Remember, these are skills and tools you can use in your daily life. As with any new skill or tool, you need practice more than once before you get all the steps down. The following questions will assist you to practice and eventually master this skill.

Each time you complete this Action Recipe, take a moment to answer the following questions.

1. When did you use this Action Recipe?

2. What part(s) do you think went well?

3. What part(s) was(were) more difficult than you thought it would be?

4. How can you tweak the action to make the activity easier for you next time?
   (List 2 or 3 ideas)

5. When can you use this Action Recipe in your life?
   (List 2 or 3 ideas)

#7 Find A New Favorite

One of the biggest obstacles to compassion is complacency. At some point in our past, we discovered what we like, and we stuck with it. People change. New things are invented and introduced. Preferences change. This task is all about letting yourself discover and rediscover things you enjoy. You've already challenged yourself to do something you enjoy, now it's time to explore something new which could be an undiscovered favorite.

Prep Time

Time needed to schedule exploration into your day.

Action Time

5 minutes to an entire day. This activity takes as much time as you choose to invest in the activity.

Steps

1. Decide you want to re-explore some of your favorite things and discover a potential new favorite.
2. Pick something you enjoy.
3. Write down 3 different versions of this favorite thing or activity.

4. Dedicate time to exploring each new version compared to the favorite in one day, or spread the process out over an entire week. For the longer discovery set aside a bit of time each day for 4 days to compare different versions of this favorite thing or activity to determine which is your favorite. Day 1 – 3: the new versions, Day 4: the original favorite.
5. Take notes as needed about the differences.
6. After trying all of these versions, determine the winner.

Benefits to Trying this Action

One of our basic needs is the need to play. This engaging aspect of ourselves gets buried as we take on more and more responsibilities in the world. Filling our own needs can be scary stuff. One of the best ways to strengthen our dedication to being compassionate with ourselves and others is to explore our current favorites. Experiencing and discovering new sources of joy is a quixk way to reenergize.

If you need ideas about which new favorite to look for, consider the following favorites.

A New Favorite Hot Beverage.

Many people enjoy a hot cup of coffee or tea each day. When was the last time you changed the contents of that cup? If you have been making it yourself, experiment with the recipe.

If you buy your beverage each day, try a different version of your favorite concoction from the same place, or go to different cafe and order the same thing you order from your regular place.

A New Favorite Fragrance.

Aromatherapy is an entire section of eastern medicine dedicated to the way smells affect us. In a harried world, this sense is commonly ignored. If you enjoy smells, head on over to a flower garden in season, and find a favorite smell. More of a city dweller, go to a store specializing in scents and find something you enjoy. If you are already a lover of scented items, try out similar scents from different suppliers to discover if your favorite supplier of that scent is still your favorite.

New Favorite Pen.

Alright, I'll admit it. I love office supplies. I am a pen kleptomaniac. I had a favorite pen type which helped me all the way through high school. The perfect pen which fit my hand, made smooth skip free lines, and spilled out ink in my favorite shade of blue was discontinued. This crushing blow was discovered the October after I started college. The loss of a consumer product was a "small thing" to other people, but this loss was a huge final loss to me. I felt as if I'd lost my only friend, again. It hurt. A kind classmate suggested, "find a new favorite". After much grieving, I did.

Every year there are two things I revisit to find possible new favorites. The first is which pen comes closest to my old favorite. The second is which farm stand sells the best vanilla ice cream in my area.

You've come to your patterns, because you discovered that these behaviors worked for you. But those behaviors may not be as energizing as they once were. Try something slightly new, and see if this tweak to your day gave you a boost. The boost is what you are after.

Where You Can Use This

You can use this technique of discovering a new favorite when the joy of your old favorite is wearing thin. Such as:
- Your favorite item makes you frown.
- Your favorite item is no longer available.
- You can't remember why something is your favorite.

Where to Avoid Using This

You should refrain from using this technique when of finding a new favorite when doing so would cause pain. Such as:
- Sitting down to a meal in a strange restaurant with an over tired child or adult.
- Joining a dating services if you are already married and your spouse has not agreed to an open relationship.
- Finding a new addictive substance after breaking the habit of the old one.

Action Review and Practice

Now it's your turn. Remember, these are skills and tools you can use in your daily life. As with any new skill or tool, you need practice more than once before you get all the steps down. The following questions will assist you to practice and eventually master this skill.

Each time you complete this Action Recipe, take a moment to answer the following questions.

1. When did you use this Action Recipe?

2. What part(s) do you think went well?

3. What part(s) was(were) more difficult than you thought it would be?

4. How can you tweak the action to make the activity easier for you next time?
   (List 2 or 3 ideas)

5. When can you use this Action Recipe in your life?
   (List 2 or 3 ideas)

One kind word can warm

three months of winter.

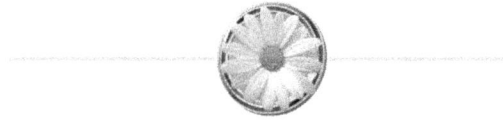

Japanese Proverb

#8 Stay in the Moment

We all have an inner critic. At times, this critic can get very loud. Sadly, the louder this inner voice is, the less it sounds like us, and the more it sounds like all the people who have hurt us in the past. One method for blocking that voice, and communication in general is to zone out, or mentally remove yourself from the surroundings. Staying in the moment, being aware of what is happening around you is important to opening lines of communication and healthily expressing yourself. This is also a fantastic way to reduce an anxiety attack.

Prep Time

None.

Action Time

10 - 20 seconds.

Steps

1. What are 5 things you See? (eyes)
2. What are 4 things you Feel? (skin)
3. What are 3 things you Hear? (ears)
4. What are 2 things you Smell? (nose)
5. What is 1 thing you Taste? (tongue)

Benefits to Trying this Action

We seldom realize when we are slipping out of the moment. Instead, we find out we have zoned out when confronted by another person or remember we intended to do something else. If you find this happening more often than you find helpful, you need to practice being present.

There are many reasons you may zone out. All are a form of self-preservation by mentally removing yourself from a situation when your physical body cannot escape. The problem with the habit of is that once we discover how well it works to avoid pain, we start to use it for every version of pain and discomfort we encounter. Staying in the moment allows us to recognize the need behind the pain. Once the need is identified, we can fill it and remove the pain instead of avoiding it.

Common Results

Forgot to Try.

Learning takes effort. Learning a new tool to replace one that is already working for you takes even more effort. The effort needed may seem like a complete waste of your time and energy. From where you are, this suggested activity probably is. You have a lot going on, with many responsibilities demanding a piece of you. Try walking through the steps when you are alone in a safe place. When you can make it through all 5 senses in a familiar place, you will be able to use this tool in more difficult situations.

Many women in my classes found it difficult to remember this technique. One brilliant woman realized she would pick at her fingernails as a way to zone out. She wrote the number five on the palm of her thumb as a reminder to try this instead. It worked for her and other women she shared it with.

Too Irritated to Continue.

You tried, but everything irked you and worsened your mood. Great information! If you tried this technique, but found the outside world, too irritating to continue, this means you are battling your brain. You have decided to make a change to improve some aspect of your life. But your brain, the sole purpose of which, is to learn from experiences and thus keep you alive, sees your new skill as subversion of a critically necessary survival tactic. Yes, your brain is dramatic. It knows all your buttons and it will use them to keep you exactly where you are, because in this instance you are still alive and thus "safe". The irritation was your brain's attempt to demonstrate how painful subverting the techniques it knows how to use can be. Those irritations are your brain warning you of imminent death from this new technique.

If you have made it partially through the 5 senses, but pulled up short in irritation, try again in a safe place. Those irritations will be there. When they pop up, thank yourself for your honesty, and ask if there is anything else. "Good job, me. See anything else annoying out there?" Make it a game with yourself to trick your brain into following along.

Something Amazing Happened.

Every moment of the day, we are each on our own path. Along that path amazing things occur. Much of the time, we are too distracted by something to notice the small seemingly magical moments. When you take a moment to silence your inner critic and be aware of your surroundings great things start to happen. Maybe you found a coin on the street, or you recognized an old friend in the crowd. Maybe you found the item you had been looking for. Or, maybe you noticed a sliver of rainbow from refraction of light off the window which was bothering you a moment before.

This process will help you find joy in the current moment. If you are currently operating under the survival tactic of not being present, this new skill may be difficult to use out in the world. That is okay. Use it in the safety of your own home at night lying in bed staring at the ceiling while everyone is asleep. That is where I started using it.

Where You Can Use This

You can use this technique to stay in the moment when you want to connect with the people and place around you. Such as:

- Going for a walk outside.
- Sitting down for a meeting at work.
- Feeling the tightness of an anxiety attack

Where to Avoid Using This

You should refrain from using this technique of remaining in the moment when you would perform better by distracting yourself from the moment. Such as:

- Mile 20 of a marathon.
- While being tortured.
- A very long car ride with annoying people.

Additional resources for this Action Recipe are provided in Chapter 6 to assist you in creating positive changes in the real world.

Action Review and Practice

Now it's your turn. Remember, these are skills and tools you can use in your daily life. As with any new skill or tool, you need practice more than once before you get all the steps down. The following questions will assist you to practice and eventually master this skill.

Each time you complete this Action Recipe, take a moment to answer the following questions.

1. When did you use this Action Recipe?

2. What part(s) do you think went well?

3. What part(s) was(were) more difficult than you thought it would be?

4. How can you tweak the action to make the activity easier for you next time?
   (List 2 or 3 ideas)

5. When can you use this Action Recipe in your life?
   (List 2 or 3 ideas)

A kind gesture can reach a wound that only compassion can heal.

STEVE MARABOLI

#9 Look for the Humanity in Others

Despite the automated world around us, we are not machines. We are living beings with hopes, fear, dreams and challenges. When we find this common connection as a species, we can be a bit more patient with ourselves and others. When you accept your own humanity, you can recognize those pieces in someone else.

Prep Time

None.

Action Time

3 to 30 seconds (faster with practice)

Steps

This is skill we need when our critiquing of ourselves and others is stopping us from progressing forward. Once this skill becomes engrained, you will find you use it in every conversation as a starting point. Things are easier when you start a conversation here. If you are not used to seeing the humanity in yourself or in others, it is best to start over in the middle of a conversation.

1. You feel your levels of irritation raising.
2. Look around to determine the source of irritation.

3. Figure out which unmet need has triggered this irritation.
    a. If the source of the irritation is:
        i. A statement someone made.
        ii. An idea in your own head.
    b. What about the statement irritates you?
        i. Person's perceived expectations
        ii. Your own expectations
4. Ask for clarification, "What did you mean when you said/did __."
5. Remind yourself the other person is human, just like you and can have bad days.
6. Listen for what underlying need their words are trying to express.

Benefits to Trying this Action

Remember, irritation in you and other is a sign that needs are not being met. When you notice the irritation, you are realizing you have a painful need that just got poked. Instead of attaching the person metaphorically poking you, remind yourself that this person irritating you, being any version of cruel, is a person. We all have problems, needs, and because of this, we all have bad days.

Common Results

Lots of Bad Days.

Just because someone is having a bad day, does not mean they are a jerk. If someone seems to have more "bad days" in your memory than "good days", then you are dealing with someone who believes you are a safe target for their anger. You do not need to take this. Use those steps for a healthy conversation to state what you need – safely. If their statement requires any action from you in order for them to stop their expression of anger towards you, you are dealing with an abuser. Leave. They are unable to meet your needs or support you in your path of Offensive Compassion.

Everything is Irritating.

Your brain is trying to keep you alive. There is something your body and mind desperately need to sustain life at the level you are demanding. Irritation, anger, and any other outburst of energy means you brain is having trouble getting your attention to fix the horrible problem which will kill you. When was the last time you had some water? When was the last time you had real food, protein, vegetables, starches, fruit? How long has it been since you had a full night's sleep? When was the last time you had 10 minutes to yourself outside of the bathroom or doing some miserable choir?

Recovering Perfectionists.

It is okay for others to have bad days, but you, you don't get to use that cop-out? Do you need to be doing things properly all the time, better than everyone else, just to be taken as normal and equal to them? Or are you just better and deny yourself these luxuries of the common people to have bad days? You my friend are a perfectionist. You've figure this out already, and have found stopping the perfectionist tendencies is the only thing you continue to fail at. You are not failing. You are learning. You are not a machine, no matter how appealing being a machine seems, being human is actually all you get. Be compassionate with yourself; you'll get more done.

Where You Can Use This

You can use this technique to look for the humanity of others whenever you are near a human being. Such as:
- Looking in the mirror.
- Waiting in line.
- Milling around in a crowd.

Where to Avoid Using This

You should refrain from looking for the humanity of others whenever you are dealing with a machine. Such as:
- Navigating the automated feature of a help desk.
- Writing a report with a computer program.
- Using a treadmill.

Action Review and Practice

Now it's your turn. Remember, these are skills and tools you can use in your daily life. As with any new skill or tool, you need practice more than once before you get all the steps down. The following questions will assist you to practice and eventually master this skill.

Each time you complete this Action Recipe, take a moment to answer the following questions.

1. When did you use this Action Recipe?

2. What part(s) do you think went well?

3. What part(s) was(were) more difficult than you thought it would be?

4. How can you tweak the action to make the activity easier for you next time?
   (List 2 or 3 ideas)

5. When can you use this Action Recipe in your life?
   (List 2 or 3 ideas)

Whether you think you can or you cannot – either way, you are right.

HENRY FORD

#10 Use Cheat Sheets

Life is an open book test. No matter how you prefer to learn, you will be tested. Use reminders for the new information and tactics you want to use. Learning takes time and practice. Cheat Sheets can help you practice the new skills through the hard parts until they become a habit.

Prep Time

3 to 5 minutes (more depending on how artistic you want to be)
1. Get paper and a writing instrument
2. Copy steps for the skill you are learning onto the piece of paper
3. Store the paper where you can get to it quickly during the day.
    a. Inside a pocket, wallet, or shirt sleeve.

Action Time

30 seconds

Steps

1. Recognize the moment as an opportunity to use the new skill.
2. Pull out your cheat sheet for the steps needed to practice the skill.

3. Follow the steps you listed.
4. Congratulate yourself for recognizing the moment and trying.
5. Put the cheat sheet away in the location you can find it when needed again.

Benefits of Trying This Action

Anyone who survived the American Public Educational System has strong opinions about the term "cheat sheets". This maligned tool is barred from most educational institutions, and half the people using them get caught and punished. Half, because we can all point to instances and people who used the forbidden tool successfully while other were caught and made an example of. If you were one of the unlucky souls who were made the example, congratulations on reading this far.

Using cheat sheets outside of the public school system is allowed. And you already use them. All those sticky notes attached to your work station, or electronic reminders set on your smart phones are types of cheat sheets. Cheat sheets are reminders. You are allowed reminders for anything you want to remember.

Some great skills to create cheat sheets out of are:
- The 5 Steps of Healthy Communication
- Your top three favorite stress relieving activities
- The items you want to remember to purchase at the store

Common Results

Forgot the Paper.

This will happen. You made a cheat sheet, because this is new information or stuff you have not mastered. You may not have recognized the moment as an opportunity to use the cheat sheet, or you many have actually forgotten the slip of paper you jotted your cheat sheet on. Either way, give yourself a break.

If you forgot to use the info, write down a few more cheat sheets with the same information on them, and stow them were you will bump into them throughout your regular day. Writing information down make it stick in your brain more quickly. That way, you are more likely to recognize the moment you could practice this skill and have a cheat sheet handy when you need the help.

Used it, but didn't feel authentic.

Any new skill you learn is going to feel weird until it is integrated into your life. This is especially true for learning a new way of communicating and interacting with the world. Remember, your brain has one job – Keep you alive! Any new skill must pass the "Will it kill me?" filter before it can be used for the first time. This inauthentic feeling is a way your brain keeps you in your known patterns. Your brain knows the current habits you use will keep you alive, no matter how painful that life is. Your brain doesn't know if this new way will hurt more, so it will be reluctant to exert the energy required.

Decide how you want to be in the world. Decide how much you want this new skill as part of your tool box. Then keep going until you can use the new skill well without looking at your cheat sheets.

Someone asked for a copy.

The first time this happens, you will be surprised by the request. It means the other person recognized this new skill you are using is helping you, and they want the benefit, too. This is true even if the person demands your copy and/or steals it from you. Congratulate yourself on learning and keep going.

Cheat sheets work best if you write them yourself. But, not everyone starting a new skill has the time or motivation to write out their own cheat sheet. That is why we have made the most popular cheat sheets available as free downloads at www.OffensiveCompassion.com. You can send them over to the website to get their own free copy, or you can help them make their own.

Where You Can Use This

You can use this technique when you want to learn a new skill, something is keeping it from sticking in your tool box. Such as:

- Having a difficult conversation with someone who as hurt you.
- De-stressing after a difficult interaction.
- Preforming a complicated task you have messed up before.

Where to Avoid Using This

You should refrain from using this technique when pausing to reference a reminder would put you in danger. Such as:

- Taking a test where cheat sheets have been banned.
- While being evacuated via helicopter from a natural disaster.
- Crossing a busy intersection on foot.

Action Review and Practice

Now it's your turn. Remember, these are skills and tools you can use in your daily life. As with any new skill or tool, you need practice more than once before you get all the steps down. The following questions will assist you to practice and eventually master this skill.

Each time you complete this Action Recipe, take a moment to answer the following questions.

1. When did you use this Action Recipe?

2. What part(s) do you think went well?

3. What part(s) was(were) more difficult than you thought it would be?

4. How can you tweak the action to make the activity easier for you next time?
   (List 2 or 3 ideas)

5. When can you use this Action Recipe in your life?
   (List 2 or 3 ideas)

Progress is impossible without change, and those who cannot change their minds cannot change anything.

GEORGE BERNARD SHAW

#11 Allow Yourself to Learn

Learning is a process. This process happens more quickly for some topics than others. Many times, people don't learn at the speed they want to, and then assume they can't learn. Everyone who gives themselves enough time and practice will eventually learn whatever topic they want to master.

Prep Time

Varies. Time needed to discover the topic exists. Multiple exposures to the topic may be needed before it breaches your awareness as a topic people can learn.

Action Time

Varies. Depending on proficiency you want to reach. The more exposure to the topic and practice using the information in your life the more proficient you will become.

Steps

1. Find someone who has mastered the skill you want to learn.
2. Model what the chosen expert does.
3. Figure out which parts are the most important for your life.

4. Focus your energy on learning the new skill and integrating it into your life.
5. Practice. Practice. Practice, and more practicing even when it seems like you are not getting anywhere.
6. Challenge yourself and ask for feedback from people who have been using this skill longer than you.
7. Keep going until you can do this skill as well as you first imagined.

Benefits to Trying This Action

Learning can be broken down into four competency levels. Much like Maslow developed the idea of a hierarch of needs in 1943, Noel Burch came up with a hierarchy of competency in 1970's.

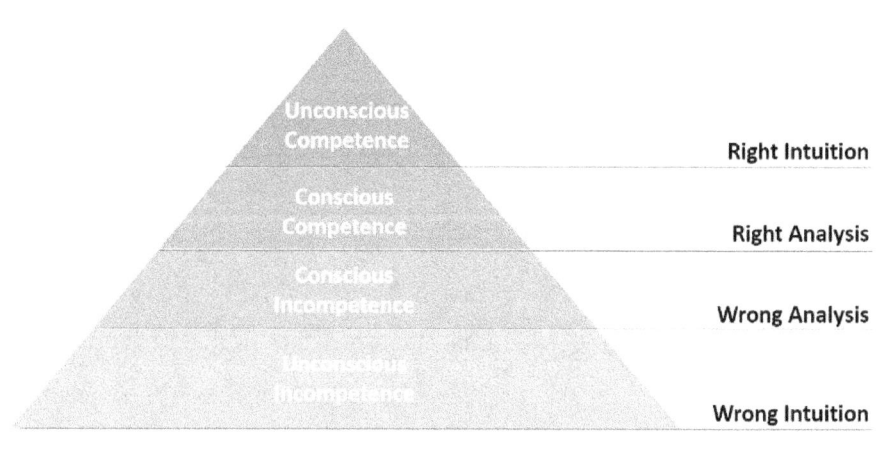

HIERARCHY OF COMPETENCY

Unconscious Incompetence.

Before the topic has breached your consciousness as a "learnable skill", you do not understand nor know how to do something. This lack or recognition means you don't realize you cannot do the skill well or at all. The brain likes this stage, and will try denying the usefulness of the new skill the first few times the new topic is presented. We must realize our own incompetence, and the value of whatever the new skill is, before we can start to learn. Some models call this stage "pre-learning", because you are not mentally able to learn the skill yet.

If you have ever sat concentrating on what someone said, but draw a complete blank on what the person just said, you have unconscious incompetence on whatever topic they just exposed you too. You did not hear them, because your brain said, "Nope. Doesn't fit." Then your brain threw out the information.

Conscious Incompetence.

This is the painful part of learning. You realize there is something out there you do not do well and realize you need to do this skill better, but it's not working yet. Mistakes are part of learning. Mistakes are practicing the skill. The only way to get through this stage of learning is to practice and keep practicing. Test yourself and ask for feedback from people who are better at this skill than you are. You can get through this painful stage if you keep going.

Conscious Competence.

You've learned a new skill, and can execute the steps well, but those steps still take concentration. You know this new skill and when to use it. This is a skill you can do, but can't multi-task through yet without goofing something up. Keep practicing. It will get easier.

You can tell if you are at this level of competence by being interrupted while preforming a new skill. If you try to multi-task listening to the interruption while doing the new skill, but get tripped up in either or both activities, you have learned the skill to this level. You still need to concentrate to successfully finish the new skill.

Unconscious Competence.

This is the stage of learning the experts are at. You perform this skill almost as a reflex, so multi-tasking this along with something else is easy. What might not be easy is explaining how you do skill to someone else when they ask for guidance.

There are two ways to learn things.
- *Intrinsically* – you have been doing this skill so long, you forgot how and where you learned it. If an expert learns the skills through innate family knowledge or behaviors, they may look at you stunned, not even realizing what they are doing has value.
- *Extrinsically* - If the expert has learned this skill with conscious effort, they may look at you stunned that you believe them to be an expert in the skill. Learning anything extrinsically, means you have broken down the steps and therefore can articulate the process you used.

Common Results

Super motivated at the beginning.

You can't convince your brain to try something new, if there is not burst of energy in the beginning. Many people start off strong and burn themselves out. Use your super motivated beginning to make a plan for the low points. Set tangle targets that will show you are progressing. Schedule in times to practice alone and with a group. Then tell people about your new endeavor. All of these boring tasks done at the beginning of learning a new skill will help to keep you going during the "hard parts" which come right after the super excited beginning.

You want to quit.

Learning is hard, because you are fighting your brain. Every new skill challenges your brain to work harder and distracts it from its one job to keep you alive. Eventually, the endorphins released at the start of a new experience will wear off, and you will be stuck in the abyss of working at a difficult skill while seeing no useful results.

Your brain wants you to quit and go back to the way you behaved before, because your brain knows these habits and skills kept you alive. Your brain does not want to risk its winning streak with anything new, no matter how painful your current life is. You are alive. That is good enough for your brain. Your brain has really good techniques to stop you just before you get the undeniable proof your new skill works better than the old one. Here are the five most common ways your brain will stop you from learning something new. You believe:

- You ran out of time/don't have time
- You run out of money/don't have enough money
- You're not serious about it/changed your mind
- You lose interest/just a fad
- You get scared/it's too hard

You will believe this internal warning, because part of you saying this. To get through, remind yourself why you wanted to learn this new thing, and make a game of catching all the excuses your brain is giving you. Reward yourself for staying on the learning curve with each interruption.

Stop and Starts.

No one is perfect. And anyone who has succeeded at anything has moments when they did quit. Not permanently, but for the day, the week, a month, or maybe an entire year…decade? The longer you wait before trying again, the more likely you are to never go back. This is your brain keeping you alive. Try again, but this time smarter. Look at where you tripped up last time and what supports you can put in place to help get over those difficult places where your brain was super unhelpful.

Where You Can Use This

You can use this technique when you want to acquire a new skill. Such as:

- Speaking a different language.
- Using a new computer program.
- Communicating with yourself and others.

Where to Avoid Using This

You should refrain from using this technique when you want to stay ignorant of the new information. Such as:

- How many antibiotic resistant microbes are in your town.
- Which celebrity is doing what and where.
- When walking through a highly classified location without the requisite qualifications.

Action Review and Practice

Now it's your turn. Remember, these are skills and tools you can use in your daily life. As with any new skill or tool, you need practice more than once before you get all the steps down. The following questions will assist you to practice and eventually master this skill.

Each time you complete this Action Recipe, take a moment to answer the following questions.

1. When did you use this Action Recipe?

2. What part(s) do you think went well?

3. What part(s) was(were) more difficult than you thought it would be?

4. How can you tweak the action to make the activity easier for you next time?
   (List 2 or 3 ideas)

5. When can you use this Action Recipe in your life?
   (List 2 or 3 ideas)

Courage doesn't always roar.
Sometimes courage is the quiet
voice at the end of the day saying,
"I will try again tomorrow."

MARY ANNE RADMACHER

#12 | Prepare for Tomorrow

The last act of compassion and self-care you can take for the day, is to prepare yourself for tomorrow. This is one habit which will show its benefits within minutes of you waking up the next day.

Prep Time

2 to 5 minutes to decide what will make tomorrow easier for you.

Action Time

10 to 15 minutes (Use a timer.)

Steps

1. Look at your plans for tomorrow.
2. Decide what you can do quickly today to save yourself frustration or time tomorrow.
3. Set a timer.
4. Do those items which would make tomorrow easier or more enjoyable.
5. Get up the next day and appreciate how your past-self took care of your present-self.
6. Pay the gift forward for your future-self tomorrow.

Benefits to Trying this Action

Even if you are a fly by the seat of your pants non-planner, there are things you do prepare. You stock food in your home for when you get hungry. You have clothing which you clean expecting to wear the items again in the future. And we all groom ourselves to our level of comfort before interacting with society. This idea of preparing for tomorrow is not foreign to any of us. What is foreign to many is preparing specifically for yourself and doing items which only you will benefit from directly.

The boost you get from these simple actions will follow you throughout the day and radiate to those around you. Good things seem to pile on top of good things before. Preparing for tomorrow gives you a base of good things to start a new pile on. If something does go horribly off the rails during your day, you can look at the small things you prepared and know you did something right. You can do more things right for yourself tomorrow, too.

This good piling on good, and conversely bad needing the reminder of good, is exactly why new recruits to the military are forced to make their beds perfectly. They are preparing for bedtime. This way, even if their day was a huge personal failure, they can see the bed made and know tomorrow is a fresh start.

Common Results

Preparations become a punishment.

One way to sabotage yourself in your preparations is to over prepare for your following day. Some people take this prepare for tomorrow concept and turn it into a punishment by creating a list of items they "must" complete before bed to "properly" prepare for tomorrow. If your preparations take longer than 15 minutes, you have too many items. If your preparations reduce the number of hours you allocate to sleep, you are doing too much. These preparations are to set you up for success the following day. If your preparations are undercutting your success with stress or exhaustion, you are not preparing yourself, you are punishing yourself.

Stop digging the hole, and allow yourself the easy path. You know you can walk the harder path. You do not need to prove your ability to do the hard stuff to anyone, especially not yourself. Try the easier path tomorrow. Imagine how much farther you could go.

Your plans change too much to prepare for anything.

This is a common complaint for people wanting to fix things in their lives, but seriously have too much chaos around themselves to contemplate how this chaos could be soothed. You will survive the night. Which means, you will wake up tomorrow and get through your day. The tasks and situations may change moment to moment, but you do not.

You are a constant, and as a steadfast constant in your life, you require things to continue on. Food, clothing, sleep, a reminder you are loved. Simple tasks such as deciding what clothes you are going to wear tomorrow, laying out breakfast items to save yourself the hassle of finding them before coffee, filling the coffee pot so you just need to hit start, or collecting all the things you need to drag out the door with you into one spot before going to bed can save you hassle and moments. Along with time, these actions comfort. Someone is helping… your past-self helping your present-self. Give yourself the gift of caring for yourself like you care for others. One small act of love will help tame the chaos.

The preparations are gone in the morning.

You prepare to make tomorrow better, but no matter how late you set your preparations up, they are missing by the time you need them the next day. You don't live in this world alone. You cohabitate, or you work with others. And those others have seen how helpful and useful those preparations you made are and took them to help themselves. They might have even thanked you for the tiny act of love your thoughtfulness gave them. Before you quit preparing and hurt yourself or these other people, talk to the other people, and find out what they need. Show them how to prepare for tomorrow and help them form this useful habit for themselves.

Where You Can Use This

You can use this technique of preparing for tomorrow any time you plan on being alive the following day. Such as:
- Attending a big meeting at work.
- Watching your favorite television show season premiere.
- Meeting an old friend for lunch.

Where to Avoid Using This

You should refrain from preparing for tomorrow when you are hoping to fail* the next day. Such as:
- Taking a test in a subject that sucks the life from you soul.
- Quitting your job.
- Ending a friendship or relationship.

---

* Planning to fail is really preparing to change routes, but wanting an external push to achieve velocity for this new direction. Extra self-care is needed for this new exciting venture.

Action Review and Practice

Now it's your turn. Remember, these are skills and tools you can use in your daily life. As with any new skill or tool, you need practice more than once before you get all the steps down. The following questions will assist you to practice and eventually master this skill.

Each time you complete this Action Recipe, take a moment to answer the following questions.

1. When did you use this Action Recipe?

2. What part(s) do you think went well?

3. What part(s) was(were) more difficult than you thought it would be?

4. How can you tweak the action to make the activity easier for you next time?
   (List 2 or 3 ideas)

5. When can you use this Action Recipe in your life?
   (List 2 or 3 ideas)

No matter what people tell you, words and ideas can change the world.

ROBIN WILLIAMS

#13 | Set Your Intentions

An intention is a directed desire of consciousness containing the spirit of what you want to create in your life and in the world. Intentions become actions. Actions become accomplishments, and accomplishments become your life. Intentions are not solid plans, but guiding themes to help guide your actions through a day or a project.

Prep Time

None.

Action Time

2 minutes of meditation

Steps

1. Sit quietly, breathe deeply, and quiet your mind.
2. Once you've found the calm awareness inside, state your intention as a positive statement.
3. Feel the joy of this outcome.
4. After you have felt the joy, you can do whatever it was you were doing before you sat down.
5. Once back out in the world, release the expectation of how this intention will happen in the world.

6. When the possibility of taking action on this intention presents itself, take the action your higher self would take while following this intention.
7. Repeat daily or weekly as part of your regular self-care plan.

Benefits to Trying this Activity

Intention is the starting point of every dream, hope and change we make in the world. It is an innate creative power within all sentient creatures which when directed towards a specific need or want seems to magically manifest what we desire. Sounds odd, right? Only if you never thought about this topic before.

Many of us take this skill for granted, like breathing. Just like breathing this skill is working quietly in our lives. Either for us or against us. If you have notices "tons of things" going wrong in your life, you might have set some very unhelpful intentions.

Not sure what your intentions are? Here are some simple guidelines to use when setting some new intentions for yourself. Keep in mind, intentions are not a stiff plan, but more of an idea that colors your actions.

Common Results

Keep intentions positive.

State or imagine your intention in positive terms. Concentrate on what you want to happen instead of thinking about these intentions as a way to avoid something. The intention: "I intend to surround myself with calm order." will work better for you than: "I intend to get rid of this clutter everywhere." The first is positive and will assist you to achieve the goal while the second has negative connotations and will stall you at every available turn.

Let intentions grow with you.

Every day we are learning and growing with every experience. Your intentions need to evolve to keep the energy behind the intention clear. If you have been using: "I intend to surround myself with calm and order." For a few weeks, and things are starting to get harried again. Tweak the intention to something like: "I intend to enjoy the calm I have created around myself." Nothing radically different. Instead, the change is a small enhancement to the original intention to make it fit better into your new environment.

Remain present.

Intentions are wonderfully powerful things which can help us achieve any goal we set for ourselves. Big intentions may take a longer time to work their way into your life. Set smaller intentions you can witness manifest in a shorter time period that grow into the bigger intention. This will make the bigger dreams come true faster. You can set long term intentions like: "I intend to start an artist colony and fully fund the artists in my home town." This is a big intention, and can become a reality. First though, you'll need to reach smaller milestones. Set an intention to reach those earlier milestones such as to meet talented local artists. Once you have accomplished this intention, set another in line with the overall intention.

Where You Can Use This

You can use this technique of setting your intentions any time you are about to interact with someone or work on a task. Such as:
- I intend to manifest happiness.
- I intend to listen to what is being said before I respond.
- I intend to lead by example.
- I intend to forgive myself and others.
- I intend to act with compassion and dignity towards others.

Where to Avoid Using This

You should refrain from setting your intentions if those intentions will intentionally cause pain. Such as:
- This day is going to stink.
- Wishing someone were dead.
- Hoping your neighbor gets hurt.
- Expecting something bad to happen to yourself.

Action Review and Practice

Now it's your turn. Remember, these are skills and tools you can use in your daily life. As with any new skill or tool, you need practice more than once before you get all the steps down. The following questions will assist you to practice and eventually master this skill.

Each time you complete this Action Recipe, take a moment to answer the following questions.

1. When did you use this Action Recipe?

2. What part(s) do you think went well?

3. What part(s) was(were) more difficult than you thought it would be?

4. How can you tweak the action to make the activity easier for you next time?
   (List 2 or 3 ideas)

5. When can you use this Action Recipe in your life?
   (List 2 or 3 ideas)

You cannot wake a person
who is pretending to be asleep.

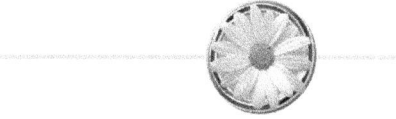

Navajo Proverb

#14 SET HEALTHY EXPECTATIONS

We all have needs we are working to fill. Yet, in certain situations our needs are unable to be met or can only be partially met. In these situations, it is important to set healthy expectations, so you are not dependent on someone else for your emotional well-being.

Prep Time

2 to 10 minutes before an encounter

Action Time

Prep time plus time required to hold healthy boundaries via healthy communication steps.

Steps

1. Before an encounter with a person or an event ask yourself these questions:
    a. What needs do I have for this encounter / meeting / event?
    b. Is this other person/are these other people physically or emotionally able to help me achieve this?
    c. Where are these other people able to help me?
    d. Where are these other people unable to help me?

  e. How will I meet my needs during this meeting / encounter / event?
  f. What quality you I want to keep in mind while achieving this?
  g. What is my exit strategy?
2. After you answer these questions, go experience the encounter keeping your expectations in mind.
3. Use healthy communication strategies.
  a. Use cheat sheets if needed.
  b. When you rub up against a need someone cannot help you will, accept it and move on. You have a plan to meet your own needs.
4. Use your exit strategy when appropriate.
5. After the encounter, take a few moments to celebrate your achievements and meet the needs which remain unfulfilled.

Benefits to Trying This Action

  Expectations are the things that get so many of us worked into a state of anger, sadness or rage. Expectations help us to survive in the world and assist us to interact with our environment. On a sunny day, we expect sun and dress appropriately. On rainy days, we expect rain and dress appropriately.

  Expectations are very helpful when we are dealing with the non-living things in the physical world, but can be disastrous when we use expectations with people.

  Let's assume you need to commute into work via public transportation. Every morning, you take the 7:15 AM train into work and the 5:23 PM train home. There is a schedule, and you arrange your day to accommodate this pattern. You expect the trains to run every day when you need them. One morning, the 7:15 train is canceled, and you need to wait for the 7:35 train to get into work. This throws your whole morning off. The first time this happens, you are shocked. By the third time, you have started to make contingency plans, especially on days when you have important events happening at work.

People change more than train schedules. We never really know how someone's day is going. It is important to set healthy expectations with each encounter you have with people. Some people are better at social interactions than other. Some people are more emotionally prepared for hiccups in their days than others. And some people are unwilling to support any part of community connection.

When you set healthy expectations before you run into people, you will find that people and events don't rile you as much as they used to. Neither the events nor people have changed for the better. What changed is your reliance on them for your emotional validation and support. Community support and validation are wonderful, but not needed if you set healthy expectations.

Below are a few things you may discover when you start setting healthy expectations with people and yourself.

Common Results

Off the drama roller coaster.
Don't get me wrong, the drama roller coaster will still be offering rides, but by setting healthy expectations, you will be able to see where the line starts to form and avoid it. Also, you may be surprised with the people who try to drag you back onto your spot on the ride. Use the steps

for a healthy conversation with these people, and offer them a cheat sheet to play along.

Your old expectations were not as healthy as you thought they were.

This is part of learning. You are acquiring new tools which when utilized may work better than the tools you used before picking up this book. If you practice setting healthy expectations and discover that previously, your expectations were not what you would set now, congratulate yourself. You have learned something new, and are choosing to use this new information. Until it is integrated into your life as a habit, there will be some slip ups. You are practicing. Keep going, and don't let the you from the past negate the better choices you are making now. We all grow. It's okay to change into more of who you are.

Plans change.

You are learning new skills and practicing them. This makes you more aware of the events and behaviors of people around you. You may find that you start to change your plans to interact with people at different times when you are more able to deal with their drama or potential requests of you. This happens when you start to recognize your needs and prepare yourself beforehand. It is part of self-care, but also about setting healthy expectations. Do what you need to do to take care of yourself and your needs. Then you will be available to truly help others.

Where You Can Use This

You can use this technique of setting healthy expectations whenever you are about to meet or interact with people known or unknown to you. Such as:
- Having a lunch meeting with a difficult co-worker.
- Visiting a friend who has just suffered a tragic loss.
- Discussing a problematic subject with a family member.

Where to Avoid Using This

You should refrain from using this technique of setting healthy expectations when tossed into a surprise event where specific pre-planning is impossible. Such as:
- An earthquake
- A tornado
- A car accident

We never know when an unexpected tragedy will occur. Instead of preparing specifically for any of these. Try to set general intentions for your day and keep those preferred behaviors in mind amid the tragedy.

Action Review and Practice

Now it's your turn. Remember, these are skills and tools you can use in your daily life. As with any new skill or tool, you need practice more than once before you get all the steps down. The following questions will assist you to practice and eventually master this skill.

Each time you complete this Action Recipe, take a moment to answer the following questions.

1. When did you use this Action Recipe?

2. What part(s) do you think went well?

3. What part(s) was(were) more difficult than you thought it would be?

4. How can you tweak the action to make the activity easier for you next time?
   (List 2 or 3 ideas)

5. When can you use this Action Recipe in your life?
   (List 2 or 3 ideas)

#15 Use Empathy

Empathy is action informed by the emotions of others. Merriam Webster Dictionary defines empathy as the action of understanding, being aware of, being sensitive to, and vicariously experiencing the feelings, thoughts, and experience of another of either the past or present without having the feelings, thoughts, and experience fully communicated in an objectively explicit manner. Empathy is not mind reading nor is empathy compassion.

Prep Time

Empathy can be used at any moment without preparations. If you do not have your basic needs of food, sleep, and safety met, expressing empathy will be exceptionally difficult. Take the time required to meet your basic needs on a regular basis, and empathy will flow easily.

Action Time

2 minutes

Steps

1. Decide you will use empathy in a given situation.
2. Listen to what the person is saying in order to understand the comment not for which response you will make.

3. Use the steps of a healthy conversation while you also consider the other person's:
   a. body language
   b. word choice
   c. tone
4. Let the other person know you are hearing them with nods of the head and small vocalizations like, "oh", "ya" and "Uuhum".
5. Take a few seconds to process what the person has said by running it through the steps of a healthy conversation.
6. Respond in a way which shows you understand what the other person is trying to convey even if their words did not clearly express that underlying need.
   a. Ask for clarification if you are unsure of what the other person needs in the situation.

When you master empathy, you do not need to use words. This means empathy is the perfect tool for traveling or interacting with people who speak different languages.

Benefits to Trying this Action

The biggest resistance I have encountered when people start to use empathy, is apathy. Why bother? What's in it for me? Empathy in itself has nothing "in it for you" beyond creating a healthy society for you to share with others by being a contentious human being instead of a selfish asshat. If that is not a big enough reward for you, here are some ancillary benefits you can experience from using empathy regularly.

Using empathy, you can:
- Understand people around you better both at work and at home;
- Have resolved interpersonal conflicts;
- Predict how your unspoken communication of body language and subtext will be received by others;
- Expect the actions and reactions of those around you;
- Be "in tune" with those around you in any situation; and
- Motivate others to create the positive impact you always wanted to make in the world.

Empathy is helping to meet someone else's needs. Helping other is its own reward. If you are aching to have your basic needs met, empathy can be a challenge, but the effort is worthwhile. All it takes is one person to make that change and be kind. Be the kindness you want to see more of in the world. It will get better.

Common Results

Empathy is exhausting.

Practicing empathy can be exhausting. If you are exhausted, you have used empathy with a person who does not want a shared experience, but is using the shared experience to control and manipulate you. If you find opening yourself to the emotions of others is draining, you need to set personal boundaries. Listen to what the other person is saying. Are they going in circles and not open to providing the clarifications you requested? Are they trying to blame others or you for their emotional state? These are not your problems and speak to the person's motivations. They have told you who they are. Believe them and set appropriate safeguard to preserve your sanity, energy and goals.

People just start taking to you.

This happens a lot. People encounter others willing to listen so rarely that when they do come across someone who will really listen, the words flow. Gender plays no roll in this expression. Empathy is a way we connect with others. When we connect with empathy, conversations are easier. You will find people opening up to you and sharing extremely interesting information and experience. This means you know how to listen to others.

You are using empathy, but not getting what you want.

Anything in this book can be twisted into a manipulation technique. Empathy the most. If you are using empathy and discover you are not getting what you want, you are keeping score. Empathy is not about keeping score. Noticing if another person is draining you is different from realizing you are not going to get what you want from the other person. If you are using empathy in the hope of acquiring something from this other person, you are weaponizing your connection. Stop it. Stop talking, and stop your toxic attempts at connecting. Go home and figure out what you need and how to meet your own needs. Only then can you reenter society as a contributing member instead of a painful leach.

Where You Can Use This

You can use this technique for practicing empathy in any social situation. Such as:
- Attending a party with friends.
- Attending a party with strangers.
- Sitting on the bus.

Where to Avoid Using This

You should refrain from using empathy when you are:
- Keeping score or feel entitled to something the other person has.
- Trying to convince someone to act against their best interests.
- Experiencing pain or probably would by opening up emotionally to someone.

Action Review and Practice

Now it's your turn. Remember, these are skills and tools you can use in your daily life. As with any new skill or tool, you need practice more than once before you get all the steps down. The following questions will assist you to practice and eventually master this skill.

Each time you complete this Action Recipe, take a moment to answer the following questions.

1. When did you use this Action Recipe?

2. What part(s) do you think went well?

3. What part(s) was(were) more difficult than you thought it would be?

4. How can you tweak the action to make the activity easier for you next time?
   (List 2 or 3 ideas)

5. When can you use this Action Recipe in your life?
   (List 2 or 3 ideas)

#16 Take a Moment to Be a Hero

Every media source loves to say our world is busy, and that we are mindless cogs in the industrial wheel with no time, money nor energy to bother with the masses around us. Offensive Compassion disagrees. It takes a moment of awareness to be a hero by preforming random acts of kindness.

Prep Time

A true random act of kindness happens instantly during the normal progress of your day. Larger premeditated acts of kindness take varying levels of preparation.

Check out the worksheets and gameboards available for download on the website, titled Take a Moment to Be a Hero, for some great ideas you can used to spur your own creative kindness and share Offensive Compassion with the world.

Action Time

5 seconds to 1 hour. Try to preform one random act of kindness a day. It will energize you and help you be more present in your daily life. (Time needed depends on what amount of kindness you want to share with the world.)

Steps

1. Decide to invest a small amount of time to be a hero by preforming one random act of kindness today.
2. Go out into the world.
3. Preform one random act of kindness.
4. If someone catches you being kind, say nothing.
5. Carry on with your day as if nothing happened.

Benefits to Trying this Activity

One small action from you can change the trajectory of someone's day and life. Take that moment to do something kind for a stranger, friend or family member. It is worth the time investment whether that investment is the 5 seconds you used holding the door for the person behind you, or the morning you spent volunteering at the community food drive.

Random acts of kindness do not need to be huge affairs costing hundreds of dollars. Not everyone can afford to walk into a toy store around a holiday and settle all the accounts on layaway. But you can still take a moment and be a hero. Here is a small list to help you see all the opportunities to be kind.

- Bring a welcome gift to new neighbors.
- Make homemade food to a struggling parent.
- Bring shopping carts back to the designated area.
- Bring treats to share with the office.
- Compliment a stranger.
- Donate books to the local library or bookstore.
- Donate clothes and shoes you don't want anymore.
- Donate your blood.

- Help a slow person cross the street.
- Help someone carry groceries to the car.
- Help someone change their flat tire.
- Let a car merge in front of you with a smile.
- Let someone else take your seat on public transportation.
- Let someone go in front of you at the cashier.
- Let someone take your parking spot.
- Let your friend vent and listen to their problems.
- Pick up litter and put it in a trash can.
- Praise a child to the parents while the child is present.
- Praise the work of others.
- Return a lost item to the owner.
- Sit with someone who is eating alone.
- Smile at people.

Common Results

You couldn't find anyone to help.

If you couldn't find someone to help, you are not preforming a random act kindness. Think about all the things you can do when no one is around. Put a piece of trash in the trash can. Recycle a bottle. Leave a sticky not with a compliment or a kind thought for someone to find in the bathroom or on a door. Heroes don't do things for the reward. Heroes are kind because it is the right thing to do. Being kind has its own reward. Be kind for yourself, and you will find more and more ways to share your kindness with the world.

You had so much fun you didn't want to stop.

Let's face it, when you remember how great it feels to help people, you won't want to stop. If you have an appointment planned, it is easier to stop than if you have a long lonely day ahead of you. For those of you with appointments, challenge yourself to continue the random acts of kindness during your appointment. For those of you with a long lonely day ahead, do a kind thing for yourself and invite a new friend.

Other people started helping, too.

People are naturally kind. It is the world which beat that kindness down. When people see someone being kind, people remember this wonderful natural state, and want to reconnect with this part of themselves and their community as a whole. Let others join you. Encourage their contributions and enjoy this random act of Offensive Compassion.

Where You Can Use This

You can use this technique of taking a moment to be a hero any time you are feeling down and need a boost. Such as:

- Not really feeling like attending the meeting? Get some treat for the people attending with you to make it a bit more enjoyable.
- Heard your co-worker comment they need a mechanic to fix the check engine light in their car? Recommend a mechanic you trust.
- Shopping in a store and see a little kid turn one way and the adult the other? Tell the child and/or adult where their companion is.

Where to Avoid Using This

You should refrain from committing random acts of kindness when that act will hurt you. Such as:

- If the house is on fire, don't clean the dishes in the sink. (Get outside.)
- If you are running so late you are about to be fired from your job, don't let people cut ahead of you in line.

Some people will say there is never a time not to choose kindness. If you are willing to get injured to help someone else, go for it. If you are not, that's acceptable, too. The point is to be kind where *you* can be kind.

Additional resources for this Action Recipe are provided in Chapter 6 to assist you in creating positive changes in the real world.

Action Review and Practice

Now it's your turn. Remember, these are skills and tools you can use in your daily life. As with any new skill or tool, you need practice more than once before you get all the steps down. The following questions will assist you to practice and eventually master this skill.

Each time you complete this Action Recipe, take a moment to answer the following questions.

1. When did you use this Action Recipe?

2. What part(s) do you think went well?

3. What part(s) was(were) more difficult than you thought it would be?

4. How can you tweak the action to make the activity easier for you next time?
   (List 2 or 3 ideas)

5. When can you use this Action Recipe in your life?
   (List 2 or 3 ideas)

#17 Make Eye Contact

There are many techniques to help make eye contact. Some eye contact can be very creepy and aggressive while others are awkward and uncomfortable. There is a middle ground which builds community and expresses acceptance. That is what you are shooting for as part of actively using compassion.

Prep Time

None.

Action Time

2 to 4 seconds when not in a conversation.

5 to 10 seconds while chatting

Steps

1. Relax. Loosen your shoulders.
2. Notice the world around you.
3. When you encounter another person out in the world, look at their face.
4. Imaging saying to them. "Hello. Thanks for being out in the world, too."
5. Smile.
6. Carry on with what you were doing.

Benefits to Trying this Action

Making eye contact is the first step in building a strong community. Before we interact with the people around us, we must notice the people around us and acknowledge both of our spaces in the world. Making eye contact is a quick way to share your community with others.

Common Results

You couldn't do it.

Let's face it. If you are not in the habit of looking people in the eye, making eye contact is an emotionally tall order. But this is a necessary step for building community and using compassion in the world, so you need to start. How? Build up to looking at the face. For a day, notice the colors of the shoes someone is wearing. Then, the next day, notice the color or fabric of their clothing. Next time out in the world, notice the color of people's hair. Finally, count noses. Smile when you count to one. Sounds silly, yes. But it works, and you are looking at people. Once you are comfortable counting noses, count noses then count eyes. Smile and silent tell these people, "I see you also have two eyes and a nose."

Note: If someone does not have two eyes and a nose, smile and silently tell these people, "I see you are human, too."

People glare at you or shift away from you.

So, you made eye contact and the other person glared back at you or moved out of the way to avoid you. This means you are being aggressive. Something in your regard had threatened these people with physical injury. Look at your intentions while making eye contact. Were you silently greeting people and appreciating the randomness of life which brings us all together? Or were you silently judging someone? Did you decide their clothes were wrong? Did you decided the other person should have groomed themselves more before running into you today? Each of us has been conditions with brief instantaneous thoughts when seeing someone. Look at your impressions of people. Those impressions are judgements. What value do these impressions add to the world? If your only answer is that it makes you feel superior to the rest of the world, you need to work harder at finding common ground with those around you.

Creepy person is following you.

One of the risks we take when interacting with the world around us is running the risk of interacting with someone who threatens us. First of all, if you feel threatened, creeped out, uncomfortable or any other personal waring that you are in some way unsafe, you are right. The other person is giving off some nonverbal micro-aggressions or overt aggression you are reading. Square your shoulders. Look at them directly in the eye. Then say out loud, while maintaining strong eye contact, "Hello. I notice you are (insert what they are doing). Is there something you need help with?"

Why this works: You are being assertive without being aggressive which allows you to defuse the situation. Your words are not aggressive, but the eye contact could be. You are letting the person who is being aggressive know that you will stand your ground. If the other person is looking for a fight, you have just signaled you are not looking for a fight, but will give one. You are not the easy target they are looking for. If the other person is not being intentionally aggressive, but instead is unable to read social clues, you have defused the situation and opened a conversation. Remember, you do not owe anyone a conversation. You can easily leave the conversation with, "I can't help you with that."

Where You Can Use This

You can use this technique of looking someone in the eye when you encounter people in your day. Such as:

- Ordering your morning coffee.
- While being interviewed.
- While shopping.
- When you encounter a sad person who needs help.

Where to Avoid Using This

You should refrain from looking people in the eyes when doing so would be really bad idea. Such as:

- Coming across a murder scene in the woods with the murder still there. (Run/Hide.)
- Running into an angry wild animal on a hike. (Not human, but eye contact can be interpreted as aggression across species. Avoid it.)
- When your gut tells you to hide.

Action Review and Practice

Now it's your turn. Remember, these are skills and tools you can use in your daily life. As with any new skill or tool, you need practice more than once before you get all the steps down. The following questions will assist you to practice and eventually master this skill.

Each time you complete this Action Recipe, take a moment to answer the following questions.

1. When did you use this Action Recipe?

2. What part(s) do you think went well?

3. What part(s) was(were) more difficult than you thought it would be?

4. How can you tweak the action to make the activity easier for you next time?
   (List 2 or 3 ideas)

5. When can you use this Action Recipe in your life?
   (List 2 or 3 ideas)

If you think you are too small to make a different, you have never spent a night with a mosquito.

Proverbs of Various Countries

#18 GIVE A GENUINE COMPLIMENT

Praise and accolades draw groups together. A large problem in our society today is that much of our praise is insincere. Taking the moment to offer a genuine compliment to another human being is a tiny action you can take to let others know you see them and appreciate their path.

Prep Time

None.

Action Time

10 seconds.

Steps

1. Be aware of your surroundings.
2. Notice something you enjoy or want more of in the world being done by someone else.
   a. Someone offering a random act of kindness
   b. A pop of color on a dreary day.
   c. A frazzled person taking the higher path
3. Instead of telling your friend about how great something is, turn to the person who did this admirable thing, and complement them on the thing that brightened your day.
4. Be specific with your praise.

a. "I really love the color of your coat."
b. "Great job getting that report in."
c. "You handled that really well. Thank you for the example."
d. "Thank you. I really appreciate you help."

Benefits to Trying This Action

There are many good things hiding quietly in this world. Notice them, and when you uncover on of these wonderful gems, make a point to compliment the person creating the thing you appreciate. Being kind in a cruel world is difficult. Being gentle in a harsh environment is an act of resistance. Offering a genuine complement to someone who is also trying to be compassionate in this world lets them know their actions are helping more than the recipient of their choices and actions. Kindness creates a ripple effect of good in the world.

The world is a large anonymous place for far too many of us. Being kind and compassionate is not rewarded in the American society. Therefore, those who accidently reveal this beautiful part of themselves in the harsh world imagine no one is watching. When someone, you, notice and call attention to that brief moment of greatness, people have varying reactions based on their levels of society involvement. Below are a few reactions you many find while out in the world giving genuine compliments.

A word of warning: Your compliment is not genuine nor appropriate if you are commenting on the person's physical appearance, social skills, intelligence, or political affiliations, or how you feel while seeing them. All of these topics, are not about the other person and instead reflect your

Action Recipes

personal biased. Before injecting your goodwill into someone else's life, check to see if you would appreciate that comment, or if you would take it as a compliment if you heard it 100 times a day.

Here are some common statements people believe are compliments, but really perpetuate the violence in our society.

Hidden Insult	Restated as a Compliment
"You have beautiful eyes."	"Have a great day."
"You are really well spoken."	"You handled that better than I could have. Thank you for the example."
"It makes me happy to see young people getting along."	"That was a very kind thing you did. Thank you."
"It's great to see an old person not be so self-absorbed."	"That was a very kind thing you did. Thank you."

When in doubt, use my favorite. "Great job." Smile and walk away.

Our society has become very violent with our use of language. When we give compliments, we have been conditioned to offer encouragement to other in a way which hurts all of us. Break yourself of this unconscious bad habit.

Common Results

Stunned silence.

Strange for you, yes. More so for the person who hears a genuine compliment. This might be the first time the person has received a compliment or a kind word. Or you might have complimented them on something others criticize them for. If you encounter the stunned silence, smile and move along. They need time to digest the words.

Dodge and run.

A step up from stunned silence is the response of dodge and run. This reaction comes when someone has been "caught being nice." They do not know how to receive a complement, or they might not believe you are sincere. People who dodge and run have been ridiculed for what you just witnessed, but they keep it up. If you encounter the dodge and run, smile and carry on.

Start a conversation.

The opposite of the dodge and run response is the start of a conversation. This happens when the person you have offered a compliment to hears the compliment, but has not learned how to accept or distinguish a genuine compliment from false ones. They are seeking to "pay you back" for your random act of kindness. This is not necessary. If you encounter the start of a consecrations and do not want to chit-chat, you can get out of the conversation with a simple, "Great seeing you. Have a wonderful day." Smile and walk away.

Thank you and walk away.

People are out and about living their lives while doing good in this world just like you. Some do it so often they have created or grown into the healthy place this activity is trying to create in you. When someone offers these healthy people a genuine complement, they receive the comments with a simple thank you and carry on with what they were doing before you and your existence intervened. If you encounter the thank you and walk away, let them go. Do not follow.

Where You Can Use This

You can use this technique of offering a genuine compliment when you witness a random act of kindness. Such as:
- Someone holding the door for you.
- Someone picks up a dropped item and returns it.
- You see someone having a difficult day, but taking the high road.

Where to Avoid Using This

You should refrain from offering a compliment when your words would increase the other person's pain, or you are expecting some benefit from offering a statement. Such as:
- Commenting on a person's physical appearance.
- Comparing a person's behavior to an entire group of people.
- Expecting the person to start a conversation with you or give you some form of payment for your statement.

Action Review and Practice

Now it's your turn. Remember, these are skills and tools you can use in your daily life. As with any new skill or tool, you need practice more than once before you get all the steps down. The following questions will assist you to practice and eventually master this skill.

Each time you complete this Action Recipe, take a moment to answer the following questions.

1. When did you use this Action Recipe?

2. What part(s) do you think went well?

3. What part(s) was(were) more difficult than you thought it would be?

4. How can you tweak the action to make the activity easier for you next time?
   (List 2 or 3 ideas)

5. When can you use this Action Recipe in your life?
   (List 2 or 3 ideas)

#19 Say Hello to Your Neighbors

We all live somewhere, but we rarely know the people living closest to us. Taking the time to wave and say hello to the people in your neighborhood will build a sense of community and brighten someone's day.

Prep Time

None.

Action Time

10 - 20 Seconds

Steps

1. Go outside of your living quarters. Either outdoors if it is a single building or into the corridor if you live in a building with multiple units.
2. If you see someone, wave kindly to them.
3. Say, "Hello."
4. Carry on with what you were doing.
    a. If you only went outside to practice saying hello, go back inside.

Benefits to Trying this Action

Our society in the United States of America is very mobile. Especially after the housing crash of 2008. May communities and the families within them have been splintered and scattered. Everyone lives somewhere. In areas with quicker turnover of inhabitants or in areas with newer inhabitants, chatting with the neighbors and the possible rejection from this local group is a scary thing. Saying hello to your neighbors, and the people who you regularly see in your day is a quick method to build community and spread a bit of Offensive Compassion.

Common Results

No reaction.

You walk outside your door. Encounter a person walking past. You say hello and possibly wave, but the person continues on as if you had said nothing. There are many reasons this could have happened which do not include intentionally ignoring you. Consider this. Maybe the person didn't hear you. They could have been listening to music or ruminating on a personal task inside their head. Just because someone is walking or preforming a task does not mean they are present for communication. Shake off the disappointment of no reaction. You are not saying hi to your neighbors to strike up an instant friendship. You are saying hello to build community. Some people are so afraid of their neighbors and people in general it will take them many greetings to inspire enough comfort for them to respond.

A wave back.

You step outside of your door. Notice someone walking by, and say hello. Maybe you wave. The other person stops what they are doing for a moment and greets you with a hello, good day or even a wave. You both have taken a moment out of your days to exchange social pleasantries. More than that, you each are witnessing the humanity in each other. This is the start of building and strengthening a community.

The chatterbox.

There are three basic responses. The chatterbox response is my favorite. You say hello, and your neighbor starts chatting with you. Did you get water in your basement with this last rain storm, too? Was that your cat laying on my porch this morning? Did you see the for sale sign up the street? Have you ever made stuffed peppers in the crock pot? Your neighbors have questions and your opening the doors of communication have given them an outlet to connect. All the questions, no matter what words were used, are an expression of "You, too?" Your answers, whatever words you use, are and expression of, "Yes, me too."

Where You Can Use This

You can use this technique of saying hello to people around you anytime you are in a crowd. Such as:
- Leaving the house in the morning.
- Waiting to get on public transportation.
- In the check outline at a store.

Where to Avoid Using This

You should refrain from using this technique of saying hello to the people around you when doing so could be disadvantageous. Such as saying hello when:

- Someone is putting the last touches on their house of cards for a completion.
- The other person is being interviewed by the local news.
- The other person is escaping a burning house.

Action Review and Practice

Now it's your turn. Remember, these are skills and tools you can use in your daily life. As with any new skill or tool, you need practice more than once before you get all the steps down. The following questions will assist you to practice and eventually master this skill.

Each time you complete this Action Recipe, take a moment to answer the following questions.

1. When did you use this Action Recipe?

2. What part(s) do you think went well?

3. What part(s) was(were) more difficult than you thought it would be?

4. How can you tweak the action to make the activity easier for you next time?
   (List 2 or 3 ideas)

5. When can you use this Action Recipe in your life?
   (List 2 or 3 ideas)

If you want to go fast, go alone.

If you want to go far, go together.

African Proverb

#20 — CREATE INCLUSIVE SPACE

Everyone wants to be accepted as part of something. This instinctive need is exceptionally strong when people are trying something new, like learning a different way to get their needs met. An inclusive space is not so much a physical location, but an environment where people feel accepted enough to bring their best qualities forward. This inclusion is a great way to find creative and effective solutions to any issue at hand.

Prep Time

2 minutes to 3 days

Preparations to create this inclusive space can be as short as setting a personal intention of being inclusive when attending an upcoming activity, or as long as it takes to write down conduct guidelines and share them with the attendees.

Action Time

The process to create the space is finite. The process to maintain the promise of the inclusive space requires constant vigilance and maintenance while the activity is being conducted. With practice, other attendees will assist in creating this inclusive space and model appropriate behavior to the newer members.

Steps

Inclusive spaces are intentional spaces. They do not magically happen. Therefore, you need to prepare for the inclusion, and you need to monitor the interactions of the group to ensure everyone is holding the same intention for inclusive space.

1. Set your intention to create an inclusive space.
    a. Alone, decide how you will signal that you are a safe person to others.
    b. In a group, forward guidelines to attendees before the event and have copies ready for during the event for those who need information on what this inclusive space entails.
    c. Practice using healthy communication techniques and de-escalation techniques before the event starts including how you would refocus the group if a moment of exclusion happens.
2. Welcome everyone to the group and thank them for their future efforts to create and maintain this inclusive space you are all creating.
3. Assure newer members of the group and give more timid people a buddy who has done this before.
4. Follow the basic structure you have created in the guidelines to reach the goals set for the event.
5. Thank everyone for their efforts in creating and maintaining the inclusive environment with you.
6. Follow up with attendees with information or next steps they can take to continue to be part of this inclusive space you created.

Benefits to Trying this Action

Creating an inclusive space brings out the best aspects in everyone involved. Each person has unique gifts for and perspectives of this world. Creating an inclusive space brings out these best aspects of everyone involved which allows the uniqueness to come up with creative and effective solutions to a myriad of problems we face in today's society. From issues as mundane as what's for dinner without leaving the house to new ways to cure cancer and hate.

Common Results

Silence.

For people unaccustomed to being part of an inclusive environment, the first response when recognizing this new group is silence. As an organizer or facilitator, this silence can be disheartening. This silence is the bane of all group leaders. It will happen. It is a turning point in the group where you need to decide whether this group is inclusive or authoritative. You've read this far; your group is inclusive. This stage of group dynamics is well studied. This growing pain is also why so many group activities start with "ice breakers".

Reassure people this space is accepting of them with a simple smile and a gentle question about a topic. Give everyone one minute to write down their answer to the question. Then go around the room and ask people about themselves and their views on a simple topic.

Lots of Talking.

Once the shock of the new environment wears off, or if the attendees have experience with inclusive spaces, people become chatter boxes. Loud chatter boxes. This can be as shocking as silence when someone socially regarded as a functional mute starts discussing a topic.

Battling Experts.

Okay, facilitating an inclusive space is not all butterflies and magic rainbows. Even while creating this inclusive and welcoming environment, people still bring themselves to this space with all of their insecurities and egos. Part of the guidelines for larger more intentional gathers include language to "leave your ego at the door." This is easier said than done for many, especially if the discussion touches upon unexpected elements related to their personal trauma.

Battling Experts is when two of the attendees' voices get louder than the others in the room. The group will instinctually congregate to the two poles. Human are creatures who build social structures on hierarchal structures. An inclusive space eliminates that hierarchy, and in the absence of that structure, attendees will unconsciously seek to create one.

Battling Experts is the first step in eliminating an inclusive space. When you see this dichotomy start, remind the appointed experts about the guidelines and the purpose of the gathering. Don't exclude these charismatic people, especially if you are trying to solve a complicated problem. Get them to work together. This will make the group stronger and more inclusive.

Where You Can Use This

You can use this technique of creating an inclusive space when you are in a group of people. Such as:
- At work in project meeting.
- With your family while discussing differing political views.
- When trying to find solutions to problems while utilizing healthy communication techniques.

Where to Avoid Using This

You should refrain from using this technique of creating an inclusive space when the people you are attempting to include are actively trying to exclude others. Such as:
- At a Hate Rally. Make the space inclusive for the attendees who are supporting acceptance and compassion. Shun the hate mongers.
- When you witness violence. Get yourself to a safe location, and create an inclusive space for the survivors of the violence.

Action Review and Practice

Now it's your turn. Remember, these are skills and tools you can use in your daily life. As with any new skill or tool, you need practice more than once before you get all the steps down. The following questions will assist you to practice and eventually master this skill.

Each time you complete this Action Recipe, take a moment to answer the following questions.

1. When did you use this Action Recipe?

2. What part(s) do you think went well?

3. What part(s) was(were) more difficult than you thought it would be?

4. How can you tweak the action to make the activity easier for you next time?
   (List 2 or 3 ideas)

5. When can you use this Action Recipe in your life?
   (List 2 or 3 ideas)

#21 Express Anger and Disagreements Safely

People disagree during situations and on solutions all the time. Those disagreements can be expressed and examined without growing into an argument. Even without an argument, anger happens. Anger is a natural reaction when our needs are not met. Being compassionate does not mean agreeing with everything someone says. Nor does it mean suppressing your needs and ignoring your anger. Compassion is all about knowing you have the skills to express your differing viewpoints in a healthy respectful manner, while dealing effectively and safely with your own anger.

Prep Time

If unexpected: Daily self-care routine to have the emotional and physical reserves to deal with the stress created with an unexpected disagreement.

If expected: Time needed to set healthy boundaries, expectations and intentions prior to expected or planned interaction.

Action Time

3 to 10 minutes (depending depth of feeling)

This is the time require to express your anger and disagreement, not the time needed to reach an agreement on the topic of contention. Reaching an agreement or compromise on the topic of contention requires moving through the steps of a healthy conversation and negotiation skills. Meeting the needs prompting the anger could take days to fully satiate.

Steps

When you recognize you are becoming angry or see that someone has unexpectedly disagreed with you and/or you are getting that tingling of irritation or full on anger:

1. Stop.
2. Take a deep breath.
3. Identify the judgmental thoughts racing through your mind.
4. Connect with your feelings/needs hiding behind these thoughts.
5. Own your anger. Anger is there for a good reason and creates the surge of energy and motivation to have your needs met. Congratulate yourself on recognizing this opportunity to express anger healthily.
6. Express your feelings and unmet needs using healthy communication steps.
    a. I See/Hear/Touch/Taste/Smell…
    b. I feel….
        i. (Mild Anger) annoyed, aggravated, dismayed, disgruntled, displeased, exasperated, frustrated, impatient, irritated, irked.
        ii. (Strong Anger) enraged, furious, incensed, indignant, irate, livid, outraged, resentful.
7. Make a clear request of what you would like from the other person. Either:

      a. Restate what you heard which triggered this feeling. "I heard…. Is this what you meant?"

      b. Request a specific action to have your need met. "Will you please (insert action here)?"

8. Listen to what the other person has to say.

Benefits to Trying this Activity

People receive negative information in one of four ways. Different sources refer to these pathways to reception differently, but all agree on the basics. The last two options are better for having needs met while continuing communication. These four ways to receive negative information are:

1. To blame ourselves.
2. To blame others.
3. To feel our own needs and desires to find the source and solution. (Self-empathy)
4. To feel the other person's needs and desires to find the source and solution. (Empathy)

Common Results

Hidden blame words.

Sometimes when we are trying to use healthy communication and not blame others for our emotions, we use words without realizing the words imply we blame the other person for our feelings. We have been taught and conditioned in this society to blame others for our feeling and disappointments. Doing so gives up your opportunity to get your needs met thus relinquishing power to those who want to control you. Resist the urge to use these passive aggressive words which escalate disagreements and destroy communication.

Passive aggressive words which escalate disagreement and anger:

I feel abused, attacked, belittled, betrayed, blamed, bullied, cheated, cornered, criticized, dumped-on, harassed, hassled, insulted, interrupted, intimidated, invalidated, invisible, manipulated, misunderstood, overpowered, overworked, patronized, pressured, provoked, put-down, rejected, ripped-off, screwed, smothered, suffocated, taken-for-granted, trampled, tricked, unappreciated, unheard, unloved, unseen, unsupported, unwanted, used, violated, wronged.

Give the expression time.

Anger usually pops up when there is a disagreement. Anger means there is a need ignored, abandoned or buried inside of you. This feeling can give you insight into where the need is located. Expressing anger and the disagreements they stem from is the first step in meeting these newly discovered needs. The needs behind anger like to hide, and have difficulty expressing themselves. If these needs were easy to express and identify, you would have found a way to meet them already. Do not put your anger on a timeline or deadline. It is there for a reason. If you must abandon the conversation or expression to see to other life events, reschedule the discussion. If this discussion is impossible with the person who helped you discover this anger, sit down with yourself and figure out how to get this need met.

Ignoring anger makes it worse.

Ignoring anger means you are ignoring a need. Diminishing the importance of anger or stifling the expression of anger is denying a need which your brain sees as vital to your continued survival. Your brain has one job, keep you alive. Anger is a signal the brain is getting worried about its ability to keep your survival streak going. That is why the passive aggressive blame words escalate disagreements into arguments. Even if you can't figure out a way to satisfy the need behind the feeling in the moment, allow yourself to feel the anger, and promise yourself you will do something kind to yourself to try and fill the ignored need. If you have been in the habit of suppressing your anger and your needs, this process of healthily expressing emotions in a safe manner will be rocky. This is natural. You can do it. The rough road is worth the trip. It's better on the other side.

Rage Monsters.

In a perfect world, everyone would grow up learning how to safely express the multitude of innate human emotions. That world does not exist, yet. Nor will it in our lifetimes. That means at some point in your life you will encounter someone who is incapable of expressing themselves in a healthy manner. You may not instantly recognize someone who has not learned to express love, joy, sadness, fear, or surprise healthily. (Beyond a strange feeling of something being "off" with the person.) Unhealthy expression of anger is instantly identifiable. The reason for their anger is still an unmet need. But these people are so unable to express that need nor meet it, they have unraveled. In children, we call this melt down a "temper tantrum". In adolescence and adults, we refer to this as a "rage monster". When someone is in a rage, they are incapable of healthy communication. Do not attempt these steps. Instead refer to Offensive Compassion Task 22, Disrupt Anger Safely for dealing with this person safely.

Where You Can Use This

You can use this technique to express your anger and disagreements safely when you notice them. Such as:

- When you are blamed for something and disagree.
- Talking to an opinionated co-worker or friend.
- Interacting with strangers on social media.

Where to Avoid Using This

You should refrain from using this technique to express anger and disagreements when doing so would put you in danger. Such as:

- Confronting a Rage Monster
- Any time a person around you is threatening or conducting physical violence.

Action Review and Practice

Now it's your turn. Remember, these are skills and tools you can use in your daily life. As with any new skill or tool, you need practice more than once before you get all the steps down. The following questions will assist you to practice and eventually master this skill.

Each time you complete this Action Recipe, take a moment to answer the following questions.

1. When did you use this Action Recipe?

2. What part(s) do you think went well?

3. What part(s) was(were) more difficult than you thought it would be?

4. How can you tweak the action to make the activity easier for you next time?
   (List 2 or 3 ideas)

5. When can you use this Action Recipe in your life?
   (List 2 or 3 ideas)

Kindness is the light
that dissolves all the walls
between souls, families
and nations.

PARAMAHANSA YOGANANDA

#22 Disrupt Anger Safely

This task is the most physically dangerous activity suggested in this book. With danger comes fear. Overcoming your fear to help people can also make this activity the most rewarding. Disrupting Anger Safely is included in this book to walk you through the process which embodies the idea of Offensive Compassion to its fullest. These suggested actions below will show you how to intervene when you witness a person intentionally hurting another.

Prep Time

Consistent self-care routines are required to prepare you for the unknown and unexpected circumstances in a compassionate and responsible way. Witnessing violence is traumatic. Recovering from the trauma is correlated to your level of personal reserves. The more reserves you have, the quicker you recover from the trauma.

Action Time

1 minute to hours. This action takes as long as it takes. Do not rush these steps. There is no time limit while dealing with people in this much pain.

Steps

1. Recognize the aggression and/or unhealthy expression of anger
2. Identify the players:
    a. The *Aggressor*: Person angry and channeling their anger onto another person or group of people.
    b. The *Target*: The victim of the Aggressor's unhealthy expression of anger.
    c. The *Bystanders*: Others not directly involved in the traumatic event, but who may be experience some aspect of the Fight-Flight-Freeze Response.
3. Decide how to intervene.
    a. Passive Intervention:
        i. Record Incident on your phone.
        ii. Share video with officials and the public.
    b. Passive-Aggressive Intervention:
        i. Go over to incident.
        ii. Place yourself between the Target and the Aggressor.
        iii. Look at the Aggressor with a neutral but stern face.
        iv. Block the Aggressor from access to the Target.
        v. If the Aggressor shifts their anger to you, reflect back to them using active listening.
        vi. Ask them if that is what they meant.

vii. Continue to listen and reflect until you discover what the person is really angry about.
viii. Ask the person if they are angry about this topic?
ix. Listen.
x. Offer a suggestion that the person leave to go get that need met.

c. Active Interaction:
i. Go over to incident.
ii. Place yourself beside the Target with your back slightly towards the Aggressor.
iii. Do not show your entire back to the Aggressor. That is not a safe move. Show the back of your shoulder. This is a subtle way to interrupt the Aggressor's unhealthy expression of anger.
iv. Smile to the Target.
v. Say hello to the Target and introduce yourself.
vi. Do not introduce yourself to the Aggressor. Ignore the aggressor.
vii. Ask the Target a question about pop culture, the weather, favorite color, TV programs they watch. Anything not related to the anger rolling off the Aggressor.
viii. Keep the conversation going, even if it is one sided. Your physical presence is supporting the Target. The Target, after

getting over the initial stun of the attack, will start chatting. This is excellent.

    ix. The two of you chatting together will take some of the energy out of the Aggressor.

    x. Invite the Target to join you at another location, if the Aggressor does not leave the area.

4. After Aggressor has left the area, stay with the Target.
5. Escort the Target to a safe location. (A bench, a café, hospital, fire department or police station.) This person may be experiencing shock. Signs of shock include confusion, unresponsive, numb, shaking, crying, or experience levels of anger themselves now that the Aggressor is gone.
6. Assess if the Target is okay using the steps of a healthy conversation.
    a. Offer them a warm/cool beverage.
    b. Offer to call a friend or family member for them.
    c. Reassure the Target that there are kind people in this world.
7. When the Target is able to return to their day or asks you to leave, wish them well and depart.

After Care

Allow time for self-care immediately and intermittently for the next 24-hours to 2 months.

Disrupting the unhealthy expression of anger is a traumatic event. This activity requires aftercare for you, the target, the aggressor, and even bystanders. You are responsible for your own aftercare, and must give yourself extra self-care after the event to rebuild your reserves and deal with any hidden needs or fears exposed by your actions in the event. The number of previous traumatic events you have encountered in your life will dictate how long you require additional aftercare.

What is Anger

Anger, like any other natural emotional response, is innately important. It is only when this natural reaction is stifled, ignored or suppressed that things get dangerous. All emotions will seek expression, because all emotions stem from an unmet need. The longer the need goes unmet the stronger and less controllable the emotion becomes.

Acknowledging the feeling, seeking the underlying need and filling it releases anger, much like food releases hunger. Anger is a strong motivator, and when this emotion is expressed in an unhealthy manner, trauma occurs.

Anger is a response to danger. Your brain has one job, to keep you alive. When it senses danger (physical, emotional, spiritual, financial, social) anger is created to save us. Anger also triggers our "Fight, Flight or Freeze" response.

- **Fight:** Physiological changes which prepare us to physically battle our way out of the dangerous situation. (Increased heart rate, increased blood pressure, vision acuity, *increase* blood flow to extremities and large muscle groups, reduced circulation to the digestive track, surge in painkilling neurotransmitters, *increase* in respiration rate.)

- **Flight:** Physiological changes which prepare us to quickly physically escape the dangerous situation. (Increased heart rate, increased blood pressure, vision acuity, *increase* blood flow to extremities and large muscle groups, reduced circulation to the digestive track, surge in painkilling neurotransmitters, *increase* in respiration rate.)
- **Freeze:** Physiological changes which prepare us to convincingly play dead to escape the dangerous situation. (Increased heart rate, increased blood pressure, vision acuity, *decrease* blood flow to extremities and large muscle groups, reduced circulation to the digestive track, surge in painkilling neurotransmitters, *decrease* in respiration rate.)

Being exposed to an expression of anger is, in itself, a potentially dangerous situation, and can trigger this innate protection reflex in witnesses. If someone was raised and surrounded by unhealthy emotional expression, any expression of emotion can be seen as dangerous and trigger the Fight-Flight-Freeze response. People who believe any expression of anger is unhealthy, have no personal examples of anger being expressed in a healthy manner.

How is Anger Expressed

Anger when expressed healthily, has no outward signal to witnesses that this emotion has occurred. A very perceptive friend may notice the increase in respiration or heart rate, but the average person will not be aware of it. Only the unhealthy expression of anger demands our awareness. This awareness is generally considered the "start" of the emotion, but it has been simmering ignored and unattended for a great deal of time before finally breaking through to public expression. Anger is the natural response to some form of pain.

When confronting anger in the wild, you have no idea what is the root of that emotional pain. Proceed carefully. With experience, you can pick out the root of the anger. Once the root is exposed, the painful need seeking fulfillment can be verbalized and in some way soothed.

Stage One of Anger Escape: Rage Monsters

Rage monsters surprise those around them. "Flipping out", "Like a light switch", and many more regional descriptions for the instant ramp up of emotion. Part of the surprise come because a Stereotypical Person has not registered the triggering stimuli as dangerous while the Rage Monster has.

Because of the surprise factor, encountering this in the wild is the hardest to predict. Usually, after someone has thrown this temper tantrum a few times, we realize they do not have the skills to healthily deal with their disappointments nor get their needs met in an age appropriate manner. As a society, we allow this in toddlers. But being insensitive to toddler's needs creates a society where we unintentionally allow this unhealthy expression to continue into adulthood.

WHEN ENCOUNTERING IN THE WILD: *Containment*. Do not approach. Keep others back. Allow them space to burn off the flash of angry energy before attempting communication or assistance.

State Two of Anger Escape: Picking a Fight

Stage two of the inappropriate expression of anger is because someone believes their personal space, territory, possessions or autonomy have been violated. This unhealthy expression is all about reclaiming personal boundaries, a wonderful need, but with unhealthy expression this turns into trying to provoke a fight with others.

By picking a fight, starting an argument, stirring the pot, the person is trying to pull their pain out of themselves by giving it to another person. Think of this as the "shit runs downhill" expression. The person is looking for someone weaker than themselves to steal that other person's possessions, security, hope - all in an attempt to gain those things in themselves. You can't steal happiness and security.

WHEN ENCOUNTERING IN THE WILD: *Social Ostracizing*. Blocking this person from social interaction is the fasted way to disrupt this expression. But, this anger has a root somewhere, and will erupt over and over until the person finds a healthy way of dealing with the emotion and getting the underlying need met. Everyone needs aftercare, even the Aggressor. When the angry person has stepped back a bit and stopped attacking, use the steps of a healthy conversation to figure out what they are seeing and how they believe that version of reality for them can meet their needs and goals.

Stage Three of Anger Escape: Physical Domination.

This is the slow burn of unhealthy anger expression. The Rage Monster has gotten attention, successfully transmitted their pain and helplessness to Targets by picking a fight, and now because the pain is still there, these unhealthy people have moved on to physically dominate their Targets. Physical violence is never a surprise. It is a hidden process of domination and coercion. The Aggressor takes no responsibility for their emotions. Instead they blame others, and thus need others around them to shift their underlying pain onto. Seeing others in pain make the Aggressor believe their own pain has lessened. Targets of physical violence have been groomed to believe they are responsible for fixing the aggressor's feelings, and will hide the abuse like one hides failures. Physical violence is rarely done to strangers.

WHEN ENCOUNTERING IN THE WILD: *Containment and Call for Reinforcements.* Do not approach without proper training. Keep others back. Trying to remove the Target is physically dangerous. In this stage of anger, the Aggressor believes they need this target to fix their emotions. The Aggressor does not see this Target as a person, but as a possession. Helping the Target escape will be met with the same resistance as if you broke into the Aggressor's house and store their favorite comfy chair. Also, the Target is in survival mode, and believes their needs do not exist.

Where You Can Use This

You can use this technique to disrupt anger safely when you witness anger in public if you choose to. Such as:
- Someone degrading another person.
- Someone bullying another person.
- When someone appears agitated.

Where to Avoid Using This

You should refrain from using this technique when doing so would put you of the other person in danger. Such as:
- Encountering a gun man.
- During a battle at war.
- Your inner self warns you against acting.

Action Review and Practice

Now it's your turn. Remember, these are skills and tools you can use in your daily life. As with any new skill or tool, you need practice more than once before you get all the steps down. The following questions will assist you to practice and eventually master this skill.

Each time you complete this Action Recipe, take a moment to answer the following questions.

1. When did you use this Action Recipe?

2. What part(s) do you think went well?

3. What part(s) was(were) more difficult than you thought it would be?

4. How can you tweak the action to make the activity easier for you next time?
   (List 2 or 3 ideas)

5. When can you use this Action Recipe in your life?
   (List 2 or 3 ideas)

#23 COMPASSION FLYERS

Catching sight of a kind word or clever sign makes people smile. A compassion flyer is a fun piece of paper with supportive comments, interesting factoids or kind humor displayed in areas where the public can read and enjoy it. Think of it as a love note to your community.

Prep Time

10 minutes to collect information.

Action Time

1 hour.

Steps

Creating flyers can become a huge time drain, especially if you are not comfortable with technology or you are creatively inclined. You do not need technology to create flyers, but it helps if you do. You do not need artistic skill to create a flyer. The intent of the flyer is what will shine through in this action.

1. Gather information for your flyer.
2. Put the information you want to share on one piece of paper to create a flyer.
3. Copy the first flyer to create more.

a. If you do not have a computer, a printer, nor a photocopier, you will need to repeat step 2 until you have created as many copies of the flyer as you want.
4. Take the stack of flyers and a roll of tape (masking tape or cellophane tape) out into the community.
5. Hang your flyers.
   a. Inside containers or buildings: Contact the person cultivating the information on display, and ask if your flyer can be included.
   b. Outside on public property: Affix your flyer to locations typically used for flyers with the center of your flyer situated at or just below eye level. Telephone poles, sides of buildings where other flyers are.
   c. Outside on private property: Contact the owner of the private property for permission to affix your flyer.
      i. Vehicles – For some reason, parked cars are fair game for marketing (which is what a flyer legally is). You can place your flyer under the wiper blades of a parked car. Don't do this on rainy days. If you are planning to distribute this way, use boring white paper, as other colors could stain the vehicles exterior.

Benefits to Trying this Action

Compassion is an active process. For many people, interacting with others using this new skill set is a challenge. If you are someone who has stumbled onto the concept of Offensive Compassion as a method for making the world a happier place, but don't want to interact with people yet, compassion flyers are for you.

Common Results

A giddy sense of hope.

This happens when you expand your circle of experience in a compassionate and personally enriching manner. You might find yourself smiling or humming as you hang the flyers. Other people undertaking this fun activity report laughing after their pile of flyers have been distributed in their community. Some people report feeling like "reverse criminals" putting kind flyers up to help people. However, this giddy hope appears in you, be kind to yourself.

Checking the flyers.

Leaving your compassion flyer is akin to leaving a cute little present for the world to enjoy. You may find yourself changing your daily routes in order to pass by your flyer, especially if your flyer includes tear away strips of fun. This is natural. Just be careful that you are not checking on the flyers as a way to punish yourself.

Compassion Flyers are a gift. People can take a little strip, or they can read it and move on. Seeing the strips still intact does not mean people have not enjoyed it. Intact strips mean that people who saw it were not comfortable destroying your creation by taking a strip. They left it intact for other to enjoy it, too. To encourage people to remove strips, tear one off after hanging the flyer.

Other compassion flyers displayed nearby.

When you place your first flyer, you may feel like a criminal. Offensive Compassion is a non-violent path to subvert and change the toxic interactions we have with the world around us. When others copy your flyers, or create similar compassionate flyers, you have finite proof your existence has made a positive impact on someone else's life. It doesn't matter if you have met this fellow creative person or not. What matters is the light you created in the world has ignited another light of kindness. The world is a brighter place and this additional light is out there reaching farther than you can alone. We are making the world a kinder place.

Where You Can Use This

You can use this technique to create and display compassion flyers in any place people gather or pass. Such as:

- In public transit areas.
- On a power pole.
- On a community bulletin board.
- In the breakroom of your workplace.
- On your window.
- On a yard sign on your property.

Where to Avoid Using This

You should refrain from hanging flyers when doing so is illegal or could destroy property. Such as:

- In a location where you or others would be in danger while reading the sign.
- Using brightly colored paper what could stain the surface it is affixed to.
- At a business or other private property without permission.

Additional resources for this Action Recipe are provided in Chapter 6 to assist you in creating positive changes in the real world.

Action Review and Practice

Now it's your turn. Remember, these are skills and tools you can use in your daily life. As with any new skill or tool, you need practice more than once before you get all the steps down. The following questions will assist you to practice and eventually master this skill.

Each time you complete this Action Recipe, take a moment to answer the following questions.

1. When did you use this Action Recipe?

2. What part(s) do you think went well?

3. What part(s) was(were) more difficult than you thought it would be?

4. How can you tweak the action to make the activity easier for you next time?
   (List 2 or 3 ideas)

5. When can you use this Action Recipe in your life?
   (List 2 or 3 ideas)

#24 THE KINDNESS CHALLENGE

Being kind and being nice are two entirely separate actions. Challenging yourself to be intentionally kind over a set period of time will help these new skills of Offensive Compassion become more intrinsic.

Prep Time

None.

Action Time

Moments of your day for a fixed duration of time, one day, one week, or one month.

Steps

1. Decide to challenge yourself to be intentionally kind to others and yourself.
2. Set a time frame for this personal challenge.
3. List one action you are challenging yourself to complete for each segment of the time frame chosen.
    a. One Day: Pick something quick you can do each hour you are awake.
    b. One Week: Pick one thing you can do each day.
    c. One Month: Pick one thing you can do each day.
4. Set the rules for your game.

a. Yes, kindness is its own reward. How else will you reward yourself for those moments when kindness is difficult?
5. Set a day to start and a day to finish your Kindness Challenge.
6. Keep track of your progress.
7. At the end of the Challenge, reward yourself for your commitment to self-improvement and to expressing Offensive Compassion.

Benefits to Trying This Action

There is kindness in the world. Some people have never seen it in the wild. If you are one of those survivors, spreading kindness may seem useless at first. Aesop said, "No act of kindness, no matter how small, is ever wasted."

Kindness is a ripple. The specific act may be small and of little consequence to you in the moment. But those ripples spread out supporting our community connections.

We never know what the person next to us has gone through to arrive at this very spot with us. The people around us may be working through some awful personal trauma behind a stoic smile. They might have had the worst news in their lives this morning and are still in the stages of denial to maintain their ability to function. They might have had a sleepless night caring for an ill friend. Or, they could be stumbling through the world's worst bout of bad luck. It means we should strive to be kind even to the most obnoxious and disruptive people around.

Do not confuse kindness with niceness. The main difference between being kind as opposed to being nice, is that kindness requires you to have personal boundaries and preform the random acts of kindness from a place of joy and fulfillment. When you do any act from a place of obligation, guilt or if the action is a sacrifice, you are not being kind. You are being nice which is another way of saying you are martyring your integrity for someone who is not able to appreciate your actions.

Common Results

People light up.

It doesn't happen every time you are kind, but it does happen more often than anyone really expects. Once in a while when you commit an act of random kindness, the person receiving the kindness or good deed smile in a way that lights up their entire being. These people are the silent warriors battling through something huge. Your shred of kindness just pushed them over some unseen obstacle.

You will feel like a super hero, because in that moment, with that little act, you are. Smile back and walk away like the rock star you are. And go back to whatever it was you were doing. It won't happen every time, but it will happen. Accept the thanks graciously and move on.

Giving until it hurts.

Kindness is about giving. If you have experience that amazing contact high of helping a grateful person, you are at risk of giving until it hurts. You might even be encouraged to keep giving, because you "owe someone" your kindness. Being kind to others while you yourself are hurting is a form of self-punishment. If your giving hurts, you are no longer "giving". You are "guilting". Kindness is not meant as a punishment.

Stop what you are doing for others and start an immediate item of self-care. It hurts because your needs are not being met. You are worth it.

You deserve kindness. Once you have recharged, you will be more effective in your efforts to help others.

Exhausted and excited at the same time.

You have made a commitment to be kind. You have your tracker of choice, and you may even be a few days into your personal challenge. At some point, not matter what duration of time you have selected, you will hit this wall. You will be exhausted where the thought of continuing is just too much. At the same time, you will have this burst of ideas of other action you can take to be kind. The desire to do all of them right now will be strong and overwhelming.

Stop. Take a deep breath. Congratulate yourself. This new skill of Offensive Compassion is becoming engrained into your personality. Your efforts for self-improvement are working. Before this new skill set is used as the new default setting of behaviors, your old patterns are putting up a fight to retain their position as go-to skill set. Remember, your brain has one job: Keep you alive. These old patterns are there to make your brain's job easier. Replacing a default setting is scary for the brain, even though you have seen some positive proof these new things work.

Your brain has more experience with how the old ways have worked, and this exhausted yet excited feeling is your brain checking to make sure you really want to replace the old ways. Be kind to yourself. The new skill sets will take hold.

Where You Can Use This

You can use this method of challenging yourself to be kind when you want your best self to show through. Such as:
- One your way to a job interview.
- While you wait in line at the airport.
- After you have seen something that makes you feel the world is cruel.

Where to Avoid Using This

You should refrain from committing random acts of kindness when doing so hurts you. Such as:
- Any time someone says you owe them or a third-party kindness. Kindness is not owed, it is granted. When someone says you owe kindness, they are really telling you they are hurting, and want you to fix their pain. Use healthy communication to find out what is causing them pain and offer some suggestions for them to fix it.
- Competing in a motor cross event.
- When your inner voice says this is not right.

Additional resources for this Action Recipe are provided in Chapter 6 to assist you in creating positive changes in the real world.

Action Review and Practice

Now it's your turn. Remember, these are skills and tools you can use in your daily life. As with any new skill or tool, you need practice more than once before you get all the steps down. The following questions will assist you to practice and eventually master this skill.

Each time you complete this Action Recipe, take a moment to answer the following questions.

1. When did you use this Action Recipe?

2. What part(s) do you think went well?

3. What part(s) was(were) more difficult than you thought it would be?

4. How can you tweak the action to make the activity easier for you next time?
(List 2 or 3 ideas)

5. When can you use this Action Recipe in your life?
(List 2 or 3 ideas)

CHAPTER 6
Additional Resources for Select Action Recipes

Taking action and making positive changes in the world around us can be a heady experience. It can also be overwhelming. The more you understand and identify your own needs and feelings, the more effective you will be in sharing your compassion in a healthy and effective manner.

This chapter offers a starter list of emotions and needs. Use these lists as a primer to start recognizing these in yourself. When you recognize them in yourself, you can more easily identify them in others.

List of Emotions

We all have needs out brains are trying to fill every moment of every day in order to keep us alive. Emotions show us how well our brain believes it is meeting those needs. Therefore, recognizing our emotions is a crucial step for meeting our needs and helping those around us. We all feel, but not everyone has been given words to express what we are feeling.

Below is a list of words we use when our needs are satisfied and when they are not satisfied to help you label your emotions. Once labeled, you can better recognize when a need appears and identify the actions to fill those needs before it causes pain.

Feelings When Needs Are Satisfied

AFFECTIONATE
compassionate
friendly
loving
open hearted
sympathetic
tender
warm

ENGAGED
absorbed
alert
curious
engrossed
enchanted
entranced
fascinated
interested
intrigued
involved
spellbound
stimulated

HOPEFUL
expectant
encouraged
optimistic

CONFIDENT
empowered
open
proud
safe
secure

EXCITED
amazed
animated
ardent
aroused
astonished
dazzled
eager
energetic
enthusiastic
giddy
invigorated
lively
passionate
surprised
vibrant

GRATEFUL
appreciative
moved
thankful
touched

INSPIRED
amazed
awed
wonder

JOYFUL
amused
delighted
glad
happy
jubilant
pleased
tickled

EXHILARATED
blissful
ecstatic
elated
enthralled
exuberant

PEACEFUL
calm
clear headed
comfortable
centered
content
fulfilled
mellow
quiet
relaxed
relieved
satisfied
serene
still
tranquil
trusting

REFRESHED
enlivened
rejuvenated
renewed
rested
restored
revived

Feelings When Your Needs Are Not Satisfied

AFRAID
apprehensive
dread
foreboding
frightened
mistrustful
panicked
petrified
scared
suspicious
terrified
wary
worried

ANNOYED
aggravated
dismayed
disgruntled
displeased
exasperated
frustrated
impatient
irritated
irked

ANGRY
enraged
furious
incensed
indignant
irate
livid
outraged
resentful

AVERSION
animosity
appalled
contempt
disgusted
dislike
hate
horrified
hostile
repulsed

CONFUSED
ambivalent
baffled
bewildered
dazed
hesitant
lost
mystified
perplexed
puzzled
torn

DISCONNECTED
alienated
aloof
apathetic
bored
detached
distant
distracted
indifferent
numb
removed
uninterested
withdrawn

DISQUIET
agitated
alarmed
discombobulated
disconcerted
disturbed
perturbed
rattled
restless
shocked
startled
surprised
troubled
turbulent
turmoil
uncomfortable
uneasy
unnerved
unsettled
upset

EMBARRASSED
ashamed
chagrined
flustered
guilty
mortified
self-conscious

FATIGUE
beat
burnt out
depleted
exhausted
lethargic
listless
sleepy
tired
weary
worn out

PAIN
agony
anguished
bereaved
devastated
grief
heartbroken
hurt
lonely
miserable
regretful
remorseful

SAD
depressed
dejected
despair
despondent
disappointed
discouraged
disheartened
forlorn
gloomy
hopeless

TENSE
anxious
cranky
distressed
distraught
edgy
fidgety
frazzled
irritable
jittery
nervous
overwhelmed
restless
stressed out

VULNERABLE
fragile
guarded
helpless
insecure
leery
reserved
sensitive
shaky

YEARNING
envious
jealous
longing
nostalgic
pining
wistful

List of Needs

We all have needs out brains are trying to fill every moment of every day in order to keep us alive. These needs are always with us. When they are not met, we feel pain. Compassion is exceptionally difficult to express when you are in pain. We have seven basic needs. Some needs required daily refills. Others, you can put off for a while with only mild discomfort. Discovering a few ways to fill each category is fun, and makes expressing your compassion much easier.

Our Seven Basic Needs

CONNECTION
acceptance
affection
appreciation
belonging
cooperation
community
companionship
compassion
consideration
consistency
empathy
inclusion
intimacy
love
nurturing
respect/self-respect
security
stability
support
to understand and be understood

HONESTY
authenticity
integrity
presence

PHYSICAL WELL-BEING
air
food
movement / exercise
rest/sleep
sexual expression
safety
shelter
touch
water

PLAY
joy
humor

PEACE
beauty
communion
ease
equality
harmony
inspiration
order

AUTONOMY
choice
freedom
independence
space
spontaneity

MEANING
awareness
celebration of life
challenge
clarity
competence
consciousness
contribution
creativity
efficacy
effectiveness
growth
hope
learning
mourning
participation
purpose
self-expression
stimulation
understanding

> ### *Watch Your Step*
>
> Every emotion is healthy. Every need is natural. It is how we express and fill those needs which can hurt ourselves and others.

Emotions can be messy. That is okay. The more we learn about our emotions, the more comfortable we become in expressing them in healthy and constructive ways. Each of the Action Recipes in Chapter 5 were designed to help you become more comfortable with your own emotions and the emotions of the people around you.

As you practice these new skills and techniques, remember you are working with information that is new to you. Yes, others have used it for decades, but this is new to you. You could not use what you did not have. And your family could not teach you what they did not know themselves. You have this information now. Share it.

Keep the parts that work for you. Let go of the parts which do not work for you.

To ease your discovery of what works and what does not work for you, the rest of this chapter contains sample trackers and other information to assist you in expressing your compassion in a healthy and effective manner. Electronic versions of this information are available as free downloads at www.Offensive-Compassion.com.

OFFENSIVE COMPASSION

#2 | Know Your Preferred Patterns Tracker

Directions: Use this tracker to mark your energy and emotions throughout the day. At the end of the day, look at what you have written, and answer the questions below. To track for a longer time frame, use additional pages.

Time of Day	How much Energy do you have?	How are you feeling?	What do you Need?
12:00 AM			
1:00 AM			
2:00 AM			
3:00 AM			
4:00 AM			
5:00 AM			
6:00 AM			
7:00 AM			
8:00 AM			
9:00 AM			
10:00 AM			
11:00 AM			
12:00 PM			
1:00 PM			
2:00 PM			
3:00 PM			
4:00 PM			
5:00 PM			
6:00 PM			
7:00 PM			
8:00 PM			
9:00 PM			
10:00 PM			
11:00 PM			
12:00 PM			

#4 Do Something You Enjoy Idea Sheet

Directions: Use this one page tracker to list the activities which bring you joy or may bring you joy if you did them now.

No.	Favorite	Thing	Time Needed
1.	Spot to Sit or Lounge:		
2.	Song or Sound:		
3.	Thing to Read:		
4.	Piece of Clothing that Fits:		
5.	Fruit or Vegetable:		
6.	Protein:		
7.	Starch:		
8.	Non-Alcoholic Beverage:		
9.	Stretching Move:		
10.	Color:		
11.	Smell:		
12:	Texture:		
13:	Mineral or Metal:		
14:	Animal:		
15:	Plant:		

Next:

- Look at your collection of favorites. (Add favorites as you think of them.)
- Estimate how long it would take you to complete one of these enjoyable things. (Listen you your favorite song. Find your favorite color / smell / animal in the world.)
- Write down how long you would need to enjoy this item in the far column.
- Find and experience one item on your list of enjoyable things.
- Allow yourself to enjoy them.

#5 Reduce Your Irritations Guide

Small irritations cumulate into large distractions without conscience thought. There could be hundreds of small unneeded annoyances in your life adding to your stress and difficulty doing what you want to do. Removing these unnecessary hurts in our lives opens us to the possibility of responding to others with more patience and understanding.

Use the space on the following pages to list the irritation in your life. Then separate the items into these categories:
1. Physical Environment
2. Health
3. Finances
4. Family/Relationships
5. Learning
6. Spirit
7. Contribution

After you have listed and grouped them, you can start to remove them from your life.

Try to remove one irritation from your life each week, or dedicate an hour a week to clearing irritation in one category.

From the list you made below:

Which category has the most items in it?

Which category has the least items in it?

Which was the most surprising addition to your list?

Which irritation do you think is the biggest problem right now?

What are three things you can do to fix this biggest problem?
1.
2.
3.

List of Current Irritations _____
(Date)

No.	Category	Irritation	Fixed
1			
2			
3			
4			
5			
6			
7			
8			
9			
10			
11			
12			
13			
14			
15			
16			
17			
18			
19			
20			
21			
22			
23			
24			

(Use additional pages if needed.)

#8 Stay in the Moment Sample Worksheet

We all have an inner critic. At times, this critic can get very loud. Sadly, the louder this inner voice is, the less it sounds like us, and the more it sounds like all the people who have hurt or disappointed us in the past. One method for blocking that voice is to zone out, or mentally remove yourself from the surroundings. Staying in the moment, being away of what is happening around you is important to opening lines of communication and healthily expressing yourself. Once you express yourself, you can start to fill your needs and recharge yourself. This is also a great way to reduce an anxiety attack.

	What do you **See**?	5	
		4	
		3	
		2	
		1	
	What do you **Feel**?	4	
		3	
		2	
		1	
	What do you **Hear**?	3	
		2	
		1	
	What do you **Smell**?	2	
		1	
	What do you **Taste**?	1	

#16 Take a Moment to Be a Hero Ideas

One small action from you can change the trajectory of someone's day and life. Take that moment to do something kind for a stranger, friend or family member. It is worth the time investment.

Random acts of kindness do not need to be huge affairs costing hundreds of dollars. Not everyone can afford to call up a school and pay off all the outstanding lunch bills. But you can still take a moment and be a hero in other ways. Here is a small list to help you see the opportunities around you to be kind.

Investment	What
Time	Befriend a lonely person.
Time	Bring a welcome gift to new neighbors.
Time	Bring homemade food to a struggling parent.
Time	Bring shopping carts back to the designated area.
Time	Bring treats to share at the office.
Time	Compliment a stranger.
Time	Donate books to the local library or bookstore.
Time	Donate clothes and shoes you don't want anymore.
Time	Donate your blood.
Time	Encourage someone who is working hard at the gym.
Time	Help a friend hunt for a job.
Time	Help a friend move.
Time	Help a lost tourist find their way.
Time	Help a slow person cross the street.
Time	Help rebuild destroyed homes and communities.
Time	Help someone carry groceries to the car.
Time	Help someone change the tires.
Time	Help someone with their bags or luggage.
Time	Hold the elevator door for others.
Time	Hug someone you love like you mean it.
Time	Introduce yourself to neighbors and bring baked goods or sweets.

Investment	What
Time	Let a car merge in front of you and do it with a smile.
Time	Let someone take your seat on public transportation.
Time	Let someone go in front of you at the cashier.
Time	Let someone take your parking spot.
Time	Let your friend vent and listen to her problems.
Time	Mentor someone.
Time	Offer someone a piece of gum or breathe mint.
Time	Offer to babysit your friends' kids for free.
Time	Offer to pet-sit for your friend for free.
Time	Offer to pick up your friend's children after school.
Time	Offer to take a picture for tourists.
Time	Open the door for someone.
Time	Participate in a community cleanup.
Time	Participate in a fund-raiser or donation.
Time	Pick up litter and put it in a trash can.
Time	Plan a vacation for your parents.
Time	Praise a child to the parents while the child is present.
Time	Praise the work of others.
Time	Reach out to someone you haven't talked to in a while.
Time	Read to the elderly.
Time	Recommend your favorite restaurant to a tourist.
Time	Recycle.
Time	Respond to emails or texts promptly.
Time	Return a lost item to the owner.
Time	Say "good morning" and "thank you" to public service workers.
Time	Share your umbrella with someone who didn't bring one.
Time	Sign up for a bone marrow donation.
Time	Sign up to be an organ donor.
Time	Sit with someone who is eating alone.
Time	Smile at people.
Time	Talk to someone new and make a new friend.
Time	Visit a nursing home and make a new friend.
Time	Volunteer at a shelter or a community event.

Additional Resources for Select Action Recipes

Investment	What
Time	Volunteer at an animal shelter during adoption events.
Money	Bring a homeless person some food and a drink.
Money	Buy an extra cup of coffee in the morning and give to a co-worker.
Money	Give a generous tip to your server.
Money	Leave extra time in a parking meter.
Money	Pay for the coffee for the person behind you.
Money	Pay the toll for the car behind you.
Money	Send a care package to your friends, family or a deployed military person.

#23 Compassion Flyers Ideas and Samples

Compassion is an active process. For many people, interacting with others using this new skill set, is a challenge. If you are someone who has stumbled onto the concept of Offensive Compassion as a method for making the world a happier place, but you are not ready to interact with people yet, compassion flyers are for you.

All you need is to place some supportive comments, interesting factoids or kind humor on a piece of paper and display it where the public can read and enjoy your gift.

Fun and kindness is the intent of these flyers. Keep them light hearted to brighten the day of whoever sees them. Fun tear away flyers topics include:

Fun:
- Factoids about the moon
- Terrible Puns
- Hugs
- Images associated with luck
- Clean knock-knock jokes

Kind:
- Hugs
- Images associated with luck
- Inspirational quotes

Compassionate:
- The Five Steps of a Healthy Conversation
- Fun things to do for free in your community
- Supportive and encouraging comments

Use the example flyers on the following pages as they are or use them as inspiration to create your own Compassion Flyers. You can download a template from the website www.Offensive-Compassion.com.

Additional Resources for Select Action Recipes

Free Hugs

- Please Take One -

Hug.... Hug.... Hug....

Yes.
You can.

- Please Take One -

The world is a better place with you in it.
The world is a better place with you in it.
The world is a better place with you in it.
The world is a better place with you in it.
The world is a better place with you in it.
The world is a better place with you in it.
The world is a better place with you in it.
The world is a better place with you in it.
The world is a better place with you in it.
The world is a better place with you in it.

Additional Resources for Select Action Recipes

These are Tearable Puns.

- Please Take One -

"Why is there music coming out of the printer? "The paper is jamming again!"	I dig, you dig, she dig, we dig, you dig… The poem is not beautiful, but it's very deep.	Where do cows like to go in their spare time? The Muuuuuseum.	If a wild pig kills you, does it mean you have been boared to death?	If you spent your day in a well, can you say your day was well-spent?	What did the football coach yell at the vending machine? "Gimme my quarter back!"	One pen to the other: You are INKredible.

#24 — The Kindness Challenge Sample

30 Day Kindness Challenge

- [ ] 1. Let a car merge in front of you with a smile.
- [ ] 2. Leave money in the vending machine for someone to find.
- [ ] 3. Leave an encouraging note for someone to find.
- [ ] 4. Leave a penny face up for someone to find.
- [ ] 5. Open the door for someone.
- [ ] 6. Be kind to someone you dislike.
- [ ] 7. Pick up a piece of litter and put it in a trash can.
- [ ] 8. Give a generous tip to a server.
- [ ] 9. Text a friend you haven't seen in a while and invite them to catch up.
- [ ] 10. Give a genuine compliment to three people.
- [ ] 11. Treat yourself to 10 minutes of quiet.
- [ ] 12. Let someone go in front of you at the cashier.
- [ ] 13. Bring a misplaced shopping cart back to the designated area.
- [ ] 14. Make a donation to a charity you care about.
- [ ] 15. Say "good morning" and "thank you" to five people.
- [ ] 16. Tell a street performer how amazing they are.
- [ ] 17. Donate books to the local library or bookstore.

Additional Resources for Select Action Recipes

- [ ] 18. Donate gently used clothing or home goods to a charity you care about.
- [ ] 19. Hug someone you love like you mean it.
- [ ] 20. Forgive yourself for a bad choice you regret.
- [ ] 21. Make a treat and share it with people you see.
- [ ] 22. Invite your friend to vent about their troubles and listen quietly.
- [ ] 23. Write a short thank you note to someone who has inspired you.
- [ ] 24. Compliment a child to their parent.
- [ ] 25. Have a healthy conversation with someone.
- [ ] 26. Read about a topic you enjoy for 15 minutes.
- [ ] 27. Do something unexpectedly nice for someone.
- [ ] 28. Hold the door or elevator for someone.
- [ ] 29. Run an errand for someone.
- [ ] 30. Smile to a stranger.

> What you are afraid to do is a clear indication of the next thing you need to do.

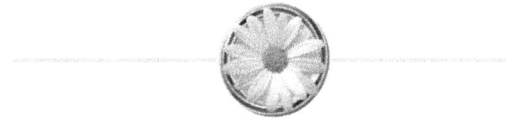

RALPH WALDO EMERSON

Chapter 7

Notes from the Other Side of Learning

The most difficult part of any journey is the beginning. All journeys must start somewhere. The journey of Offensive Compassion starts with the decision to do something to make the world a better place.

You have made it this far in the book, so you either enjoy my snarky style or you are contemplating how you, too, can actively add compassion to the world.

There is no perfect place to start. There is just the space where you do start, and it becomes the perfect starting point for you in retrospect. If you need a clearer path, I suggest starting with Action Recipe No 1. It is where I started. It has served me well.

Remember, pain makes us selfish. Pain comes from unmet needs. So, the first step, is recognizing your needs. This will start you on the path of filling your needs. When your needs are met, you have the emotional band width needed to deal with other people in a more compassionate and intentional manner.

Be kind to yourself. Your entire life, you have been using tools the way you were trained to use them. You believed you were using the tools as well as anyone could. The ideas and activities in this book may have opened your mind to the possibility that there is another way. You might have noticed some parts of this book were hard to read, because they stung too close to home. Be kind to yourself. You did not know any better way was out there.

Now that you do know a better way exists, you will need practice to make these patterns stick. Just because you know better, does not mean your brain believes in the new techniques right now. Practice is the only way to make these new skills work for you. Keep with it. Like anything else you have learned, you will learn how to express your compassion in an active and meaningful way.

Express Your Style

Communication styles are partly what we were taught combined with what we have learned, mixed with what we want to express. It is a lot like getting ready in the morning.

People feel most comfortable in public when they have groomed to their personal level of comfort. This grooming comfort level is different for everyone. That is why some people can roll out of bed in yesterday's clothes and sprint out the door ready to take on the world. While other people spend hours preening before they are equally confident in their abilities to take on the world. It is a personal preference. We call personal preferences "style". People can have styles for anything. Communication preferences are no different.

You might want to "wing it" after quickly skimming this book. Or you might want to approach Offensive Compassion in a more organized manner with notes, practice groups and peer support. Whichever way you choose to go, do it with integrity while you look for the common ground.

Hundreds of self-help book related to figuring out your communication style and how to deal with people using a different style are on book shelves across the country. They are fun to read, but you don't need them to express compassion.

When you used these healthy communication techniques to express yourself with compassion, you automatically get around the pitfalls of bad communication habits others use. When we talk about communication styles what we are really discussing is who taught these people how to communicate and the family/group dynamic these people grew up under. Recognizing these five common communication styles, may help you reach a consensus faster, or help you prepare for a difficult discussion when needed.

The Five Communication Styles

Our families teach us our communication skills. Then the groups we socialize in reinforce those patterns. You can change your patterns if they are not working for you. To do that you must recognize them first. Below are the five general styles people discover to help you identify them in the wild.

The Assertive Style

Assertive communication is born of high self-esteem or through dedicated work. It is the healthiest and most effective style of communication - the healthy balance between being too aggressive and too passive. This assertiveness gives the user confidence to communicate without resorting to games or manipulation. It is about knowing our needs while not allowing others to push us because they want or need something from us. While the most effective, this Assertive Style is the least used in the United States, because not many families used this naturally.

Common Characteristics of Those Using this Style
- Achieving goals without hurting others
- Protective of own rights and respectful of others' rights
- Socially and emotionally expressive
- Making choices and taking responsibility for them
- Asking directly for needs to be met, while accepting the possibility of rejection
- Accepting compliments

Spotting Them in the Wild
- Voice: Medium pitch and speed and volume
- Posture: Open posture, symmetrical balance, relaxed
- Gestures: Even, fluid, expansive
- Facial Expression: Good eye contact
- Spatial Position: In control, respectful of others

What You Might Hear Them Say
- "Can you please stop at the store and pick up milk? I'm stuck at work, and we are out."
- "Thank you."

What You Might Feel During and Encounter with These Users
- You know where you stand with them.
- You can trust them.
- You can share constructive feedback without personal attacks.

All of the following communication styles are variations of unhealthy communication techniques. If you recognize the patterns you used before reading this book, be kind to yourself. You did not know a better way to use this tool. When you replace unhealthy communication skills with more healthy and effective ways of communicating, it is actually easier to spot people using those unhealthy, less effective tools in the wild.

The Aggressive Style

This style is all about winning at someone else's expense. An aggressive person behaves as if their needs are the most important and/or they have more to contribute to the world than other people. This an ineffective communication style, because the information gets ignored as listeners protect themselves from the delivery style.

Common Characteristics of Those Using this Style
- Frightening, threatening, loud, hostile
- Willing to achieve goals at expense of others
- Out to "win" at all cost
- Demanding, abrasive
- Belligerent
- Explosive, unpredictable
- Intimidating, bullying

Spotting Them in the Wild
- Voice: Volume is loud
- Posture: Bigger than others
- Gestures: Big, fast, sharp/jerky
- Facial Expression: Scowl, frown, glare
- Spatial Position: Invades personal space

What You Might Hear Them Say
- "You are crazy!"
- "Do it my way!"
- "You are so stupid!
- "You can't so anything right!"
- Sarcasm, name-calling, threatening, blaming, insulting.

What You Might Feel During and Encounter with These Users
- Fight-Flight- Freeze response starts
- Uncooperative
- Resentful / Vengeful
- Humiliated / Degraded
- Hurt
- Lack of Respect for them and yourself
- Fear of retaliation or violence

The Passive-Aggressive Style

People who use this style appear passive on the surface, but are acting out their anger in indirect or behind-the-scenes ways to undermine the other person or group. People captive against their will often act in passive-aggressive ways in order to deal with an overwhelming lack of power in a given situation. These users often feel powerless and resentful, and express their feelings by subtly undermining the object (real or imagined) of their resentment. Many times, they even sabotage themselves.

Common Characteristics of Those Using this Style
- Indirectly aggressive
- Sarcastic
- Devious
- Unreliable
- Complaining
- Sulky
- Patronizing
- Gossips

Spotting Them in the Wild
- Voice: Often speaks with a sugary sweet voice.
- Posture: Often asymmetrical – e.g. Standing with hand on hip, and hip thrust out
- Gestures: Can be jerky, quick
- Facial Expression: Often looks sweet and innocent
- Spatial Position: Often too close, even touching others while pretending to be warm and friendly

What You Might Hear Them Say
- It sounds like they are agreeing, but a dig or hurtful comment is added at the end. Sometimes under their breath.
- "Why don't you go ahead. Do it; my ideas stink anyway"
- "Oh don't worry about me, I can do it by myself, like always."

What You Might Feel During and Encounter with These Users
- Confused
- Angry
- Hurt
- Resentful
- Unexplainably on edge

The Submissive Style

People using this style try to please others in order to avoid conflict. They behave as if they their needs do not exist or matter while the other person's needs are more important than their own. They are trying to fill other people's needs to force the other person fill theirs. This submissive behavior is marked by a martyr-like attitude and a refusal to try anything which could improve their condition. After a while, people start to resent the low energy surrounding people using this submissive style of communication and quit trying to help because their efforts are subtly or overtly rejected.

Common Characteristics of Those Using this Style
- Apologetic if they accidently express a need or opinion
- Avoids any confrontation
- Difficulty in taking responsibility or in making decisions
- Yielding to someone else's preferences
- Opting out while playing the victim
- Blaming others for events or problems
- Refusing compliments

Spotting Them in the Wild
- Voice: Volume is soft
- Posture: Make themselves as small as possible, head down
- Gestures: Twist and fidget
- Facial Expression: No eye contact
- Spatial Position: Make themselves smaller than others

What You Might Hear Them Say
- "Oh, it's nothing, really."
- "You choose; anything is fine."
- "Whatever. I don't really care."

What You Might Feel During and Encounter with These Users
- Exasperated
- Frustrated
- Guilty
- Start second guessing yourself
- Taken advantage of

The Manipulative Style

People who used this style have weaponized their communication skills. It involves scheming, calculating and shrewd tactics to gain control of a situation or outcome. These communicators are skilled at influencing or controlling others to their own advantage. Their words hide an underlying message, the other person is usually unable to articulate the manipulation until after reviewing the unsettling interaction later.

Common Characteristics of Those Using this Style
- Cunning
- Controlling of others in an insidious way
- Asking indirectly for needs to be met
- Making others feel obliged to solve their problems
- Unpredictable emotions

Spotting Them in the Wild
- Voice: Whatever is needed to maintain control
- Posture: Takes their own space and draws people in
- Gestures: Controlled, quick
- Facial Expression: Unsettling eye contact
- Spatial Position: Moves in and out of personal space

What You Might Hear Them Say
- "You are so lucky to order pizza. I wish I had some. I can't afford to get pizza every week."
- "Does this dress make me look fat?"

What You Might Feel During and Encounter with These Users
- Guilty
- Frustrated
- Angry, irritated or annoyed
- Resentful
- Unexplainably uneasy

Recognizing the Different Communication Styles

As you read through the last section, you might have recognized those traits and behaviors in people you know. Recognizing the five basic styles of communication will help you react effectively when confronted with a difficult person. Also, it can help you recognize areas to focus your self-improvements on.

You always have a choice of how to respond to the people around you. Start with the Five Steps for a Healthy Conversation presented in this book. Following that simple scripts will keep you in the assertive and healthy window communicators strive for. The other four styles are common ways people veer away from the structure of a healthy conversation. The quicker you recognize the common detours, the quicker you can get the conversation back on track.

Becoming an effective communicator will help you meet your needs with more ease and reliability. This ease has a side effect, a high level of self-awareness. Self-awareness can also lead to crippling self-doubt. When that happens, remind yourself you didn't know any better before you learned the difference. Now, you know the difference, you can choose your next steps.

Next steps are easiest to take after your basic needs are met. When you are talking with anyone, you have no idea how well these other people are meeting their own needs. If the person is not using the steps for a healthy conversation or assertive style, they are making their lives more difficult than they need to be.

When you encounter one of these styles in the wild, notice which blocking technique they are using, and which part of the reflexive listening worked best with people using the styles. You will find people accustomed to using one of these styles are also accustomed to ignoring similar needs or needing similar needs filled.

Encouragement for the Low Points

Our low points hurt. We reach a point where we wonder, "How much worse can it get?" Then the universe sucker punches us again, and we sink to an even worse lower spot.

We've all had low spots. The loss of a job. The death of loved one. The betrayal of a friend. The world's crappiest luck where everything went completely wrong and ruined everything. Not everyone has been homeless. Not everyone has lived in a shelter. Not everyone has lost every penny to their name. That doesn't mean your low point isn't valid. It doesn't matter what propelled us on this downward slide into a living hell. All that matters is you are in a low spot, and where you are sucks.

Annoyingly, we have all heard the stories of people who after reaching their low points sprung back stronger than before. It seems like every successful person has crawled through their personal hell to emerge on the other side living their dream life.

> *Helpful Thoughts*
>
> **An arrow can only be fired after it is drawn back.**

We all have our own versions of hell. What you find miserable, someone else might find wonderful. Your worse could be someone else's better. That is why we can't compare pain. Pain is pain. We cannot qualify the pain as more or less than someone else's.

Pain makes us selfish. When we hurt, our pain is everything to us. We want our paint to be equally important to someone else, so that they are motivated to help us relieve the pain. Pain cannot be compared, just experienced.

> *Helpful Thoughts*
> **Pain is pain, and all pain is equal.**

I didn't believe this statement until after January 16, 2008 at 7:36 AM. I cracked my skull in a car accident. My brain sloshed for months. The pain was so excruciating it recalibrated my notion of pain. I healed and regained a new normal. For a headache to register on my pain meter, it has to be a debilitating migraine.

A couple years after the accident, I started vomiting at work. My head hurt a little. My right side was bit more sluggish than it usually was for the new normal, and the florescent lights were irritating me more than usual. It was a migraine. I put on some sunglasses, took some antacids and migraine medicine. I kept working, and went home at the end of the day completely drained, unable to move.

A couple of days later, I was back at work. A co-worker, accustomed to being healthy, started to see spots. The right side of his face got numb. He couldn't drive, so he called his wife. She drove him to the emergency room. Hours later, his wife called to report, my co-worker had a migraine and would be back in the next day.

When he came at the end of the week, he asked me if I had ever had a migraine like the one he experienced. He had much more respect for the pain of a migraine after he had experienced one. But our co-workers razzed him for going to the hospital for a migraine where I had just kept working.

Our responses to pain were different, and neither of us was wrong. When people want to compare pain, they are looking for one of two things: proof the pain will end or a way to discount the suffering. Either route, they want the pain to stop.

Pain doesn't end just because you want it to. Saying someone's pain is not as bad as someone else's pain does not make the pain in either person go away. Discounting pain makes pain hurt more.

You must do something to end the pain. Pain means you need something that is missing. Finding the missing thing is the only way to remove the pain. At our low points, we realize the missing thing may never come back. That job, that loved one, that friend may be gone forever. In those miserable moments, we are at a crossroads.

> *Helpful Thoughts*
> Doing nothing is a choice.

Crossroads demand a choice, just like our low points. The longer we go without making the choice, the further we fall into a deeper low point. You can only choose from the options you see. When we are in a deep dark pit of hell, there are no "perfect choices". There are only choices that are slightly better.

In your low moments, make a choice a smidge better than you would have yesterday. Let' say you lost your job. This is a traumatic experience when you are not setting that timeline to leave. Getting another job is scary prospect regardless of what kind of job you are looking for. We hope that this change will get us into a slightly better job.

What we deem "better" is entirely up to personal preference. Someone accustomed to earning $500 a day would consider a job offering $400 a day terrible. While, another person accustomed to earning $300 a week would consider $400 a day a dream job. A third person may consider any job "better than none" if it means they can keep their home.

No matter what job someone is looking for, the process is equally stressful for all those searching.

If you've read this far, you are looking for something, too.

On my worst days, when I am stung by the many injustices in the world and the limits of my humanity, I remind myself of the one thing that keeps me going.

> ***Helpful Thoughts***
>
> **Tomorrow will come in a few hours. Do one thing to make tomorrow easier for yourself.**

We can do this together.

About the Author

Mellisa Sherlin is an internationally, award winning, and best-selling author with over 30 years of publishing credits to her name. She is currently the president of the Essex Writers and Artisans Guild of Massachusetts, a support group for creative people meeting weekly since 1991. When she is not writing or helping other writers learn the business side of creativity, she teaches women healthy communication skills to create and sustain the life they want through her work with shelters in the Merrimack Valley. Her community outreach grew into this book, *Offensive Compassion*. Always up for meeting new people, Mellisa enjoys taking her big yellow labrador retriever to the beach on dreary days and getting lost on road trips.

If you would like more information, please visit our website www.Offensive-Compassion.com and sign up for our newsletter to get more ways to express yourself delivered to your inbox.

Recommended Reading List

Armstrong, K. (2010) Twelve Steps to a Compassionate Life. New York, NY: Random House, Inc.

Evens, P. (2010) Verbally Abusive Relationship: How to Recognize it and How to Respond (Expanded Third Edition). Avon, MA: Adams Media.

Lue, L. (2003) Nonviolent Communication Companion Workbook: A Practical Guide for Individual, Group, or Classroom Study. Encinitas, CA: PuddleDancer Press.

O'Connor, J., Seymour, J. (2011) Introducing NLP: Psychological Skills for Understanding and Influencing People (Neuro-Linguistic Programming). San Francisco, CA: Conari Press.

Rogers, A. G. (2007) The Unsayable: The Hidden Language of Trauma. New York, NY: Ballantine Books.

Rosenberg, M. B. (2003) Nonviolent Communication: A Language of Life. Encinitas, CA: PuddleDancer Press.

Sherlin, M. (2017) Offensive Compassion Companion Workbook: A Practical Guide for Individual or Group Study. Lowell, MA: Cerulean Streak Media.

If you do not change direction, you may end up where you are headed.

LAO TZU

www.ingramcontent.com/pod-product-compliance
Lightning Source LLC
Chambersburg PA
CBHW070559300426
44113CB00010B/1324